Orton, William Aylott, 1889-

The economic role of the state.

THE ECONOMIC ROLE OF THE STATE

No free government, or the blessing of liberty, can be preserved to any people, but by a firm adherence to justice, moderation, temperance, frugality and virtue and by a frequent recurrence to fundamental principles.

The Virginia Declaration of Rights, 1776

THE ECONOMIC ROLE OF THE STATE

By

WILLIAM AYLOTT ORTON

THE UNIVERSITY OF CHICAGO PRESS
CHICAGO · ILLINOIS

CHARLES R. WALGREEN FOUNDATION LECTURES

THE UNIVERSITY OF CHICAGO PRESS, CHICAGO 37
Cambridge University Press, London, N.W. 1, England
W. J. Gage & Co., Limited, Toronto 2B, Canada

 Published 1950
Composed and printed by THE UNIVERSITY OF CHICAGO PRESS
Chicago, Illinois, U.S.A.

To

HERBERT DAVIS

PREFACE

☼

THIS book had its origin in a course of lectures given at the University of Chicago in October, 1948, on the Charles R. Walgreen Foundation for the Study of American Institutions. The text has since been revised and expanded, but the cardinal aim is unchanged; namely, a "recurrence to fundamental principles." That aim controls both the nature of the argument and the selection (or omission) of illustrative material.

W. A. O.

NORTHAMPTON, MASSACHUSETTS

CONTENTS

☼

I

THE ROLE OF THE INTELLECTUALS

☼

THERE died in Florida, on July 17, 1948, the author of one of the most popular parables of our time. He was an old circus star called "Papa" Zacchini, and his parable had no words. It needed none. It is known, everywhere the big top goes, as the human cannon-ball act. He had seven sons, two of whom introduced the act to New York in that wonderful year 1929. The New Yorkers acclaimed it; one might even say that they recognized it; they have been making charts and graphs of it ever since. To quote an excellent piece of reporting:

> Hugo Zacchini would crawl feet-first into a monster cannon. After a drum roll and a carefully timed pause, his brother, Mario, pulled the lanyard. "Boom," and out flew Hugo, partially wreathed in smoke, describing a graceful curve on his way to the safety net. The act was welcomed by fans, who had been complaining of a falling off in the danger content of the circus.[1]

The fans have no complaint now; but I have sometimes wished that Hugo would emerge from the smoke of battle in full academic costume and fly through the air with the greatest of ease, clutching a slide rule in one hand and *Robert's Rules of Order* in the other.

But, no; that is too lofty an image. It is down on the sawdust rather than up in the air that we intellectuals belong: God's clowns, whose job it is to keep the show going in between the big acts. The monster cannon trundles off to get set for the next performance, and out we run, upside-down or right-side up, riding pickaback on one another, walking on

1. *New York Times*, July 19, 1948.

stilts, throwing handsprings and somersaults all round the arena. Go into your act, clown, pick up that applause—and watch your timing.

We never fail. Many of us remember the letters coming in, after World War I, from colleagues in enemy lands: "Dear So-and-so, are you still alive?" Once more we are getting them; one comes to my desk as I write. It opens with the old phrase: "Well, here we are again"—which, as the writer knows, is the traditional greeting of the clowns when they reopen the circus. Here we are again, discussing the same old problems that Socrates and Cicero, Aristotle and Aquinas, discussed. One might suppose, if he were very naïve, that by this time we should have settled something; but that would imply a gross misapprehension of the Greatest Show on Earth. Perhaps it is not the function of the intellectuals to get things settled. Suppose we succeeded; then where should we be? Even intellectuals have to live—provided, of course, that they do not think the wrong thoughts or compose the wrong music. The judges of Socrates asserted that he unsettled things; and people have generally indorsed the charge but disputed the sentence. The same is true of many a successor to Socrates. Does it reflect a persistent feeling that it is just as well to keep things stirred up and to tolerate a corps of professional stirrer-uppers? The word "sophist" was not always a term of reproach; even the title "professor" has had, in both Germany and America, its moments of prestige. Are intellectuals as such, are colloquies such as this, of any real use or practical effect in the world?

As a modest starter, we may say that the function of the intellectual is to maintain that pressure of reason upon mere circumstance from which alone true meaning, for the rational animal, emerges. Obviously, that is a task that can never be finished. Only the angels, according to lore and legend, embody pure intelligence; and there are grades and hierarchies even among them. Presumably there is some sort of celestial aptitude test. Man is certainly, as Evelyn Underhill calls him, the border-line creature: never, nor even meant to be, completely rational—whatever meaning one imputes to the term. Have we not all met people so pretentiously rational that it would be a relief to throw the fire irons at them? From among such people have come the most dangerous fanatics in history.

It is from the limitations no less than the potentialities of human nature that its highest achievements arise: as it was in the beginning, is now, and ever shall be. This seminal impulse to impregnate the givenness of mortal circumstance with a life that laughs at time as well as locksmiths justifies the intellectual no less than the poet and the artist; and his justification, like theirs, is that the work is never ended. Perhaps that was why Shakespeare made a clown out of a gravedigger. More and more people, we hope, may come to share the life of reason; but that sharing means not a broader rump to sit on at the board of plenty but a stiffer backbone as we rise to face the remorseless challenge of the stars. We shall not agree with H. G. Wells that "mind is at the end of its tether" if we remember that it was precisely Wells and his forebears who cut the tether too short. He never renounced his initial assumption that the very nature of the universe, man included, is comprehensible, at least potentially, by the mind of any bright young science teacher. That assumption still inspires a good deal of modern exhortation, especially in the social sciences. But rationalism proved once again the enemy of reason, as well as of certain other virtues. Wells grew very angry with fate for chalking a rude question mark across his credo; but when he proclaimed that *Homo sapiens* is finished, we might still consider the report exaggerated.

The disillusionment of H. G. Wells and his fellow-travelers marks a significant stage in intellectual history. But not a novel one. The collapse of modern rationalism, far from negating the work of mind, merely sets it back with a bump onto firmer ground. The sins against hope, says the catechism, are presumption and despair. Having committed the one, we should be the more careful not to fall into the other. For safety's sake, let us start from a position more modest than that of Descartes, Comte, Spencer, and their vanishing progeny. Let us say simply that the effort of the intellectual to transmute mere fact into intelligibility is a distinctively humane endeavor, constituting its own justification. Naturally, we hope, and most of the time we assume, that the effort will also increase the supply of vitamins and contraceptives, books, bombs and bacteria, bread and circuses; and so far we in America have done pretty well for ourselves. But even if these gay pragmatic hopes are not all realized, the effort to render experience intelligible is still worth while for its own sake.[2] It is one of the humanest ways of killing time. It constitutes the widest and most durable plane of human intercourse, giving us more courage to go on than all the bright utopian dreams of adolescence.

Certainly the ideal of thought for thought's sake echoes the ideal of art for art's sake: a very sound and salutary ideal, especially in the circumstances it challenged and the achievements it inspired; much sounder than the ideal of art for comfort's sake, or art for money's sake, or art—I trust I do not misinterpret Signor Dali—for sensation's sake. We are compelled to wonder whether those who gibed so glibly at the ideal of art for art's sake were on such solid ground as they thought they were; whether, in fact, they knew what they were talking about. They could not, of course, be expected to know that it is ten thousand times harder to paint a good picture or write

2. "The perception of justice, the knowledge or thought of truth, artistic creation and enjoyment, possess a significance of their own, a value in themselves, even if we ignore their utility to the living being which exercises such functions" (Ortega y Gasset, *The Modern Theme* [New York: W. W. Norton, 1933], p. 43).

a good poem than to devise an improved washing machine; so they could fool themselves into believing, against all the evidence, that art was merely a species of hedonism which they could patronize or not as they damn pleased. What the artists were saying—what such artists as Eric Gill and Rockwell Kent have spent their lives in saying—is something that modern materialists do not want, and cannot afford, to hear. But in so far as we drive the Lehmbrucks and the Woolfs to suicide, we cut the veins of our own civilization. It is a question not of comfort but of spiritual significance.

The basic problem of Western man, especially European man, is to find enough reasons today for wanting to be alive tomorrow. To that problem science returns a dusty answer. Only a fool, and a fool without conscience, would promise a resumption of the nineteenth-century banquet. The last course is served, the bill is on the plate, and we are all raiding our assets to pay it. We should have had more time had we been less reckless; but war—as I pointed out twenty-eight years ago[3]—merely accelerates tendencies already in existence; it does not create them. We cannot base our hopes for the future upon a resumption of the cheap and easy living standards of the past. The economic position of humanity as a whole is not getting easier; and the relative position of the Western world, including the North American continent, is permanently altered to its disadvantage. We have to adjust our outlook and our tempers. We of the West shall not see again cheap fuel, cheap steel, cheap building, cheap automobiles, cheap meat, cheap clothing, such as we saw in the 1920's, no matter what we do. If they appear once again to be cheap, we shall pay the added cost in other ways—as indeed we are now doing. The rest of the world will level up, we all hope; but, as part of the process, we shall have to level down a bit. The habit of reflection therefore may help us meet the future with prudence, jus-

3. *Labour in Transition* (London, 1921), p. xiii.

tice, temperance, and fortitude. It may also help us to distinguish between that which is given in our environment and that which is controllable: to accept the one, and tackle the other, in reasonable humor.

There is an inherent tendency in direct democracy to overestimate the latter—the controllable part—and minimize the element of necessity. A pioneer people that has accomplished so much in the material realm is easily persuaded that there are no limits to what it can accomplish, even in short periods and in realms much less simple. But there are. History does not support the idea that the course of progress, however one define it, makes the problems of humanity simpler. The potentialities of human action are certainly enlarged; we may perhaps say (optimistically) that they are enlarged equally for good and ill; what we cannot say is that the problems and the possible solutions get simpler. It would be truer to say that the challenge to human virtue seems to keep pace with human potentiality. In proportion as any group of people attains maturity destiny gives it a man-sized job to do; and the first requirement is to outgrow the swelled-headedness of adolescence, which makes ideal tasks seem simpler than they are. The idealism will be clearer when it has been through the sieve of disillusion.

This word of caution—of conservatism, if you like—is relevant to certain phases of our present theme which will be more fully discussed hereafter.[4] One of the most striking is the propensity of all radicals to assume that much wider and deeper areas of economic life can be changed by fiat than is actually the case. Economic rationalists of the more radical sort, few of whom have ever had much personal experience of pro-

4. Some of these are acutely analyzed by Professor Frank H. Knight in a study of "The Determination of Just Wages," comprised in the volume *Twentieth Century Economic Thought*, recently published by the Philosophical Library, and edited by Professor Glenn E. Hoover (New York, 1949).

ductive processes, are a useful source of criticism of established customs and practices. But the occasions on which they have been able to take over have arisen less from the merits of their arguments than from the destruction or collapse of existing systems, as in the cases of the French and Russian revolutions. Where the historic structure of a society—not only its material equipment but its social and spiritual norms—has been wiped out, life among the ruins, if it does not become merely bestial, is likely to follow an a priori rationalism because there remains no indigenous alternative. But it would be wrong to infer from such cases that this "engineer's approach" should or could be equally applicable to societies that are still going concerns. One can "reconstruct" a machine or a skeleton but not a living organism; for the latter, as Lincoln said, the true policy is to "heal." That may imply a quite different mode of action, for it can heal (if at all) only in its own way, according to its own essential nature. We may not like that way; we may indeed, not without reason, come to despair of it; but the extent to which we can impose a different way is more limited than we are disposed to think. And if this is true of a devastated area, it is even truer of a still vigorous society such as our own.

It is significant that such able defenders of economic freedom as Knight and Hayek have recently come to emphasize the limits of Cartesian rationality as a principle of social action.[5] Both agree that the amount of economic life which is rationally knowable or explicable (in this particular way), and therefore controllable, is smaller than the engineers are willing to admit; and that, even if it were larger, there are other fac-

5. Knight, *op. cit.*, and Frederick A. Hayek, *Individualism and Economic Order* (Chicago: University of Chicago Press, 1948), chap. i. I cannot help regretting that Hayek has nailed his thesis with the term "individualism"; for what he is defending is not individualism, but classical liberalism, as against its Continental perversions. No brand of individualism ever was, or ever could be, a philosophy of freedom—as Hayek's own text abundantly demonstrates.

tors and values which cannot be ignored or dissociated. After all, the average of human happiness—if one may use such a phrase without invoking the absurd arithmetic of Bentham—is not solely a matter of the quantity of goods available, or the size, or even the distribution, of the national income.

Lord Russell, in one of his finest essays, describes mathematics as "the subject in which we never know what we are talking about, nor whether what we are saying is true." Precisely on that ground he commends it; his point, of course, being the complete detachment of the scientific attitude.

> It involves a sweeping away of all other desires in the interests of the desire to know—it involves suppression of hopes and fears, loves and hates, and the whole subjective emotional life, until we become subdued to the material, able to see it frankly, without preconceptions, without bias, without any wish except to see it as it is, and without any belief that what it is must be determined by some relation, positive or negative, to what we should like it to be, or to what we can easily imagine it to be. . . . A life devoted to science is therefore a happy life, and its happiness is derived from the very best sources that are open to dwellers on this troubled and passionate planet.[6]

All this has an obvious bearing on the role of the intellectuals. Back in 1927 the French philosopher Julien Benda published a book called *La Trahison des clercs;* had it been as effective as it was celebrated, the next two decades might have been less shameful to mankind. Benda's complaint against the intellectuals of his time (he was born in 1868) was that they had reduced, or traduced, the humanism of the Middle Ages to a set of local passions and prejudices whose ultimate clash could not fail to be spiritually as well as physically disastrous. The very ideals of truth, beauty, and justice, he pointed out (with plenty of evidence), had been subordinated to the ramp-

6. *Mysticism and Logic* (New York: Longmans, Green & Co., 1925), pp. 75 and 44–45.

ant nationalisms of the age. Apart from its prophetic quality, the significance of the work now lies in Benda's attempt to redefine the universal. In a word, his plea[7] is for disinterestedness, alike in science, art, and morals. He has no use or excuse for "that teaching according to which intellectual activity is worthy of esteem to the extent that it is practical, and to that extent alone." Such teaching he regards as a deliberate betrayal of science by scientists serving the passions of their democratic paymasters. On the political control of art, any informed reader can now supplement Benda's text. As for morals, he has this to say:

> If we ask ourselves what will happen to a humanity where every group is striving more eagerly than ever to feel conscious of its own particular interests, and makes its moralists tell it that it is sublime to the extent that it knows no law but this interest—a child can give the answer. This humanity is heading for the greatest and most perfect war ever seen in the world, whether it is a war of nations, or a war of classes.[8]

That was written during the "Locarno period"—which did not fool Benda. But to any competent student of that time, and of the years that preceded and followed it, the saddest thing is that there was never any lack of such warning.

Is it perhaps unreasonable to demand objective thinking, which almost by definition should lead to conclusions universally acceptable, when it is ourselves, individually or collectively, that we are thinking about? There are serious practical obstacles in the way, and one of the few things the modern "clerc" can do is to point them out. There are three in particular.

One is the overvaluation of political activity. We are suffer-

7. My word is ill chosen: Benda does not plead; he denounces in fine Old Testament fashion. See the English translation, *The Treason of the Intellectuals* (New York: William Morrow & Co., 1928), pp. 151 ff.

8. *Ibid.*, p. 183.

ing a veritable plague of politics and may easily come to resemble Athenian democracy at its worst. Many good people, with the best of intentions, are demanding more, not only of the average voter but of the average congressman, than he can possibly deliver in either quantity or quality of political action; and the mere machinery of government tends to make a balanced over-all view physically impossible. I doubt if there is a better analysis of this situation, and its consequences, than Walter Lippmann offered a quarter-century ago in his book *The Phantom Public*. "The man does not live," cried young Mr. Lippmann, "who can read all the reports that drift across his doorstep." And, if that was so in 1925, to what a size has the drift grown now! We are annually snowed under with hundreds of thousands of pages of printed matter, much of it unedited and unindexed, plus that rain of sleet that the general public never sees, which a clever commentator has called "government by mimeograph." On top of all this comes the professional and lay comment, with which, in at least half-a-dozen fields, a qualified observer must attempt to keep up; and, after all that, he is supposed to have ample time for reflection and independent judgment. He may sacrifice his family, his health, his hobbies, and his eyesight; but there comes a point at which he is entitled to suggest that government itself, to remain intelligible, should not bite off more than it can chew. The limits on collective endurance are certainly narrower than those on individual tenacity. Too many decisions of important issues are reached at the point where collective endurance can simply stand no more. And when we speak of the difficulty of getting an over-all view, the suspicion arises that no such thing exists: that the complexity and confusion are such that no general pattern, or contrast of patterns, is objectively there; that no "fundamental principles" are relevant because nobody is, or can possibly be, aware of them in the chaos of particulars, passions and prejudices being therefore all you can expect people to hold on to, because in fact you do not have to hold on to them, they hold on to you.

Now part of this situation certainly arises from the overvaluation of political activity as such; from the popular propensity to believe that every social problem can be solved, every desideratum attained, by making a law about it. It is a touchingly childlike faith, for, when something goes wrong in the child's environment, his first thought is that somebody (he or his father) ought to compel somebody else to do, or cease and desist from doing, something or other. Sometimes the child is right; but more often than not we have to explain that the situation is not quite as simple as that. Some of us tried to explain that to American lawmakers in the 1930's, but without much success. A more objective study of the record, and of the motivation that lay behind it, might help to correct the current overestimate of the efficacy of political action.

It might also help to improve the quality. The one matter on which most of us are capable of expressing a realistic opinion is our own interest as we see it. That is true of people acting in association even more than of people taken individually. Such opinions are the raw material of popular politics. They issue in demands, pressure groups and lobbies, on the one hand, campaign speeches and election promises, on the other. What happens after that is, in the American system of government, mostly beyond our control. But somewhere, somehow, somebody has to shape a policy out of this welter of private demands and particular interests. There is no natural harmony between them on that plane, no invisible hand shepherding them all into a spontaneous synthesis. The good of each is not the good of all, much as we would like to think so; and any popular legislature is more harassed by the former than concerned with the latter.

Must we then leave the job of synthesis to the Chief Executive, aided by whatever collection of experts and advisers he sees fit to call into counsel? Suppose the experts disagree—as at this moment both they and their critics notoriously do? Yet if the electorate, organized and unorganized, voices nothing more than a clamor of particular interests, and presses those interests (as it does) upon the legislature, the task of making a synthesis is bound to result in an increasing centralization of power. So much European experience verifies this conclusion that it is unnecessary to labor the point. If, therefore, democracy is to be made safe for the world, or even to survive in practical politics, one conclusion is inescapable; namely, that there must be a nucleus—an elite, if you like—of people who are both willing and able to evaluate the general effects of the particular interests with which they are directly concerned.

This is a most difficult requirement; but democracy is the most difficult form of government. It is a requirement that calls not only for intellectual objectivity but for moral objectivity in a degree that it is not reasonable to expect of the majority of people. Democracy, therefore, has to generate its own leadership, in the moral as well as the intellectual sphere, for ultimately, as the Greeks taught us, the two are one. That requirement presses directly upon the intellectuals, upon all who have the power and the responsibility of molding popular opinion. It concerns not only the professional talkers, teachers, preachers, commentators, columnists. It concerns corporation directors and trade-union leaders, editors of the business and the labor press, managers of broadcasting stations and newspaper proprietors, to whom the choice between self-interest and public duty is sometimes presented in very costly terms. Somebody has to bridge the gap between private interest and the general welfare; and if we the people cannot or will not do it, the state is bound to take over—whether for better or worse.

The current vogue of so-called "public opinion" polls is

none too healthy a symptom.[9] Carefully followed, such devices give a useful demonstration of the instability and the limitations of the mass mind, on the level that is accessible to their methods; but that is all. They may indicate very roughly, and for very short periods, what lines of action might find a merely arithmetic support or disapproval. But if they are taken—as they tend to be—to indicate what *ought* to be done, what policies should be, or even can be, pursued, their effects may be both dangerous and misleading. What matters most to a democracy is not the quantity but the quality of opinion. From Thucydides to Lincoln there is abundant proof of that. And the quality of opinion is the special responsibility of those who are in position to affect it.

We do not, and should not, assume that the natural leaders of opinion, doing their work as conscientiously as they can, will find themselves in spontaneous agreement on all major issues. That is neither probable nor desirable. Their proper function is one of clarification; it is to show us, in broader terms than the average preoccupied citizen can compass, what the issues really are, what choices are really open to us, what the grounds and effects of such choices may be. There is no higher service to democracy than this. On this level, if we can attain it—and from time to time democracy does attain it—objective thinking is indeed worth while for its own sake. A difficulty brought into clear focus, a problem grasped and stated in terms that admit of intelligent alternative solutions, add something of themselves to the mental and moral stature of man.

Second among the three goals of objective thinking is the extension of the current time perspective. Lord Northcliffe—Alfred Harmsworth by name, pioneer of modern mass journalism with all the pioneer's instincts—attributed much of his

9. This was written and stated a month before the elections of 1948 and is here reproduced without change.

success to his being able to guess what the man-in-the-street would be interested in two weeks from now; but not four weeks—that would have been too long. Some of the most startling developments in modern politics, and some of its brightest reputations, have been built on the brevity of popular memory. The skilled politician knows this, counts on it, and is expert at guessing when and how the underlying trends will reassert themselves, whether in his time or somebody else's. For they do have a way of reasserting themselves; so perhaps in the end the brevity of popular memory is corrected. But painfully and at too great a cost. When the League of Nations was being quietly garroted at Dumbarton Oaks, with the Americans sitting on the body while the Russians twisted the cord, no publicist remarked that that was too harsh a treatment for so young a creature. The youngster had ventured to condemn and expel a great democratic ally; we were all determined that that sort of impertinence should not occur again. Our precautions are adequate. But the entire situation might have been different had the public been taught to think of the work of the League in terms of decades or generations rather than months or years; in terms of the slow inculcation of the habit and practice of international community. The subsequent emphasis on rule-making and the machinery of coercion represents the search for a short cut by frightened people in a hurry. In matters of this magnitude there is no short cut, least of all by the method of coercion; and the brevity of the popular time perspective is therefore a serious danger.

Much of the confusion and instability in national economic policies, and even theories, of the last two decades has been rooted in a gross underestimate of the economic consequences of World War I—in some cases a wilful underestimate. Those of World War II are only just beginning to appear; and again we detect a certain reluctance to recognize their magnitude and permanence. Again we are tempted to invoke short-run remedies against long-run trends: to exaggerate, for example, the importance of loans and donations as compared with basic reconstruction; to postpone vital decisions about the latter as long as we can make shift with the palliative effects of the former. Now is the time to be on our guard against a second and a greater disillusion. If the current efforts of the International Trade Organization and the Economic and Social Council produce tangible results within five years, we shall be moving fast. If there is much to show within a decade, we shall be doing very well indeed. A sound historical perspective at the outset will save us disappointment later on.

Third of the three tasks of objective social thinking is the fight against abstraction. A. N. Whitehead pointed out many years ago that abstraction is the hallmark of common thought —and he was not using the word "common" in the complimentary sense that some of us assume when we speak of the common man. What Whitehead meant and said was that it takes a special effort of the trained intelligence to think effectively in the concrete. Popular journalism and popular politics are ridden with abstractions, because abstractions are the great vehicles of mass emotion, of emotional mobilization. As Hegel said, "Fanaticism wills an abstraction." Reality is distressingly complex; it thwarts and annoys every primitive impulse. How much simpler is the theory of economic classes than the reality of economic society! How much easier to accept the myth of the proletariat than to decide for myself the measure of my duty to my employer, my family, my neighbor! How tempting for the intellectual to freeze the flowing reality of social life in a solid block of concepts and categories! Such things are useful and necessary aids to thought; far too frequently they become substitutes for experience.

We have here a lesson to learn, and perhaps a warning to take, from the development of modern physics. The closer we come to reality, the more we must recognize that we are dealing with innumerable streams of tendency, running parallel, blending, conflicting, clashing violently; coming from origins we cannot always trace; and never lying wholly on the surface. We must recognize too—and here is the catch—that we ourselves are not standing on the banks of the river we are trying to chart but splashing about in an effort to keep our own heads above water. As the physicists say, the observer himself is part of the total situation. The validity of his observations depends on his bearing that fact in mind. For everyday purposes it does not much matter, but on critical occasions it becomes important.

The village community, with its town meeting and its local autonomy, knows by experience what its needs are, what resources it has, how and why its decisions are made, and how they work out. It is not tempted to regard itself, in its collective capacity, as Santa Claus or Superman. But, on the big scale, we all tend to think of government or the state as something out there and far away: a vast machine that does things to us or for us, but with whose operations, once having set it up, we have very little concern. So remote it seems that we easily credit it with almost magical powers, a superhuman omniscience, and an independent morality. Even when the record shows a degree of inefficiency and vacillation that would ruin any corporation director or high-school teacher, we feel no sense of personal responsibility. It is always "they" or "he" who went wrong, never "we" or "I." But the observer himself is part of the total situation.

Of course powers and responsibilities have to be delegated; so, to a large extent, do critical functions—as they are, or are supposed to be, in the party system of a free society. There remains however a certain danger arising from the abstract character of big government and its apparent divorce from the concrete experience of ordinary individuals. The rise of direct democracy and mass communication has enhanced rather than mitigated the risk. Individuals are tempted to surrender more of their responsibilities to government than is good for either them or it; and to demand more of it, especially over short periods, than it can possibly deliver.

There is an interesting connection between the rise of direct democracy and the increasing centralization of power. It is not wholly due to the technological factor. Perhaps some of the attitudes people used to assume toward an anthropomorphous deity or the Puritan "Providence" have been transferred to the modern state simply because it is big, powerful, and remote, and some sort of faith is still needed. The fact that state action minutely affects everyone does not dispel the psychological distance, because while the doings may be ubiquitous, the doer remains remote and (often literally) inaccessible. "Providence" was rather like that—remote, majestic, a little grim, but nonetheless supposed to be minding everybody's business.

We see a popular reaction to the remoteness of big government in the persistence of the spoils system and the petty graft that goes with it. Much of this springs from the instinctive effort of powerless individuals to retranslate the abstractness of government into personal terms. Wholesale denunciations often miss the point that every politician, policeman, and ward boss knows; namely, that people like some actual human agency to be for them "the law" and make it mean something in terms of their personal and family interests; injecting a little pity, charity, compassion, into what certainly ought to be an impersonal and impartial system; taking account of the frailties of human nature and the messes it constantly gets into—not only when "trouble" comes to the family but when there are electoral promises to be (more or less) made good, government regulations to be interpreted, permits or licenses to be obtained, and so on from day to day. It is all very well to protest that this personalization of government can easily lead to corruption; the term is very difficult, in practice, to define. At the local level there are many kinds of price for a vote besides a cash one, and we should be flattering ourselves if we maintained that the plane or the scale of such transactions was merely local. The power of the Fascist and Nazi movements was largely built up on this sort of thing. No government that relies for support on special interests, little or big, is on a sound basis.

In the abstract, of course, we all agree to that; but in the concrete it is not so simple. Is not the struggle of interests for political control bound to arise under any government that has a positive policy? Must not any constructive policy demand that this or that segment of the economy be encouraged and protected, this or that segment be discouraged and restrained? And if this is so, how is a battle of interests both with one another, and for or against the government, to be avoided? In that sort of struggle the intellectuals, the "clercs," the elite, naturally count for very little unless they join up with one of the contending groups and become, in effect, propagandists. One can hardly blame them if they do. Anxious to "make their contribution," they may well decide to back whatever group seems to them, as individuals, the least wrong, or the nearest to what they think is the true line. Yet if they all do that, will there not be some function lacking to society, some position betrayed, some "trahison des clercs"? On the other hand, not only is it unrealistic to expect that any considerable proportion of the populace will maintain or appreciate an attitude of sublime detachment, but the "clerc" may come to doubt whether he has either an intellectual or a moral right to maintain such an attitude himself. How can he be sure that his judgments are really objective, his sympathies truly impartial? Had he not better swing into line with one or another of the "historic forces" and abandon the futile, and perhaps unwarranted, attempt to remain above the battle?

We shall be much concerned with this dilemma in the following pages, and many readers will no doubt disagree with what this writer has to say. But on one point there will, I think, be a large measure of agreement: the dilemma is a real one.

II

THESIS AND ANTITHESIS

✲

THE conflict of interests, mainly economic, has become in modern times the central concern of both jurisprudence and practical politics, superseding the older and loftier theme of the nature and purposes of human society as such. The relations of the individual, on the one hand, and the state, on the other, to this conflict now constitute an inescapable, though still introductory, problem.

I shall argue, in the following pages, that in terms of our current aims and assumptions the problem is insoluble: that these aims and assumptions, in either their national or their international application, cannot and will not lead to social harmony or synthesis but must and will lead to increasing discord and disintegration. The aims and assumptions in question are those which are often grouped under the general term "neo-mercantilism." Their common characteristic is the view of the state as a positive and active agent in promoting the material enrichment of a politically defined society. In this view the multiplication of controls and regulations and the struggle to enforce them not only on individuals but on associations of all kinds, including other states,[1] are regarded as merely incidental to the economic ends, which are taken as self-evident. Against all this, I shall advance the following thesis.

a) The unique characteristic of the modern state is the power of coercion. Of course there is plenty of practical coercion in

1. And churches. Events in Central Europe have shown how the religious societies, Protestant as well as Catholic, are inevitably drawn into the struggle. As the argument proceeds, we shall see why this must be so.

industrial society by what are technically private associations; but the special attribute of the state is legalized coercion. This is, or should be, a reserved power, not to be invoked in the spheres of ordinary life and work however tempting its use may be. The activity of the state is bounded by the sphere of autonomous personality.

b) In practice, however, intelligent autonomous personalities (such as, no doubt, the present reader and the present writer) are all too few in this world; and even under the best of circumstances their interests will to some extent conflict. But to remedy this situation by the increase of coercion is to frustrate the natural course of development. As Hayek very usefully points out,[2] the great service of Adam Smith and his school, Burke included, was to propound a system within which ordinary people, being neither superrational nor supermoral, could pursue their ordinary motivations with a minimum of harm and a maximum of freedom. The monistic system to which Cartesian rationalism leads may (or may not) offer certain tangible short-run gains, but at the cost of deeper and more lasting losses. If a monistic type of society were needed, its center could not and should not lie on a level that excludes large and dynamic elements of personality. That is why totalitarian systems always take on a pseudo-religious character and why no true religion can get along with them.

c) The logic of materialistic state "planning" calls for government by theory rather than by principle (Hayek has the distinction of government by orders versus government by rules that everyone can understand).[3] Economic theory as a basis of state coercion has so repeatedly proved fallible, even by its own standards, that it should never, by itself, be the dominant factor. Even if we admit the unrealistic assumption

2. *Individualism and Economic Order*, pp. 11–13.

3. *Ibid.*, pp. 18–19.

that particular theories can be divorced from particular interests, we cannot assume that economic means and ends can be divorced from other means and ends, in either theory or practice. Political wisdom consists largely in understanding the connections. It is here that the "fundamental principles" enter the picture; and we shall therefore consider not merely what the principles are—as to which there is little new to be said, though plenty to be done—but what *sort of things* they are.

d) This may help to clarify the current confusion between two contrasting ideals of the state: (1) the state as the executive agent of an essentially voluntaristic community and (2) the state as the supervising engineer of a vast system in which each component is assigned its particular function with reference to a master-plan. The contrast stands whether one believes the master-plan to be sound and workable or incoherent and self-contradictory. By a voluntaristic community I mean not a community in which everyone is inspired with altruism and benevolent sympathy toward everyone else (nor did Adam Smith mean that) but a community which has *grown into* a general tacit concensus as to what is right and wrong, decent and indecent, in modes of social action. The tendency of modern times has been adverse to this kind of growth.

e) Finally, and therefore, I shall argue that the criteria and goals of state action should be primarily moral rather than economic. Subsidiary organizations may, and must, have more limited ends; but where economic ends are made primary for the state itself, the resulting rigidity and complexity of administration, and the *plane* as well as the nature of coercion, are incompatible with the growth of true democracy. The moral evaluation of policy is perhaps no simpler or easier than the economic evaluation. It certainly demands more training than is generally demanded or supplied. But it is a task less alien to ordinary human nature than pure rationalistic calculation and therefore in its very exercise tends to make the citizen a better man. It may be no easier in a specific situation to define the term "justice" than the term "common economic interest"—and in both cases an approximate and minimal definition may be as much as can be expected—but the ordinary person has more aptitude for the former task, and by working at it he may thereby get a truer approach to the latter.

Thus baldly stated, the thesis not only sounds arbitrary but does in fact prejudge certain issues that call for more consideration than can here be given. The reader should note what these issues are:

1. The previous paragraph implies a view of human nature with which many writers, ancient and modern, do not agree. What is implied is in fact the basic philosophy of natural law. This holds that there are at least latent predispositions in human nature to recognize certain broad standards of right and wrong; that these predispositions are developed by free social life; and that the standards so recognized are of universal validity. This doctrine, in its eighteenth-century form, is built into the foundations of the United States of America. Much modern teaching holds it to be fallacious. If this little work should help to revive the critical study of natural law, it will have served a useful purpose.

2. In positing morality as the proper criterion of state action, we must remember that for practical purposes there is no such thing as morality in general. We may more or less agree as to the class of rules and relationships to which the term "moral" shall apply; but that is not enough. In practice morality means this and not that set of "fundamental principles," these and not those business and social modes of behavior. In the same way, economists have to recognize that such terms as "food" and "clothing" have meaning only for abstract, mostly statistical, purposes. We do not buy "food"; we buy

potatoes, fishes, steaks, chops, cabbages, loaves of bread, etc. We do not buy "clothing"; we hunt for a particular dress or suit or coat or hat or pair of shoes. The statistical categories are merely a summation, useful for certain limited purposes, of the actions of individual persons whose differences, for other than abstract purposes, are just as "real" as their statistical identity.[4]

Now if morality is to be held the final criterion of policy, in the sense above cited, the old problem of secular versus religious authority is bound to arise; not, of course, because anyone wants to start a row, but because, since morality must be made specific, we need some agency to define it—at least in the sphere of *res publicae*. Would it not be simpler to deny that secular government has any concern with it at all? Well, in practice we have seen enough of that denial, from Machiavelli to Mussolini, to say that it does not work. More significant is the fact that systems that start out on what they call a "realistic" basis—meaning a basis of sheer expediency—speedily become the most dogmatic moralizers, as witness both Nazi Germany and materialist Russia. It is simply impossible to maintain, in either pure theory, history, or practice, that the state is by nature amoral—that is, morally neuter. But unless we hit upon the right approach to the problem, it will force itself upon our notice, as it has so often done before, in the guise of a struggle between state and church—secular versus religious authority.

Ideally, of course, there should not be any "versus," since there is no ontological distinction between man as man and man as citizen. Religious rules and sanctions cannot be fundamentally at variance with secular morality if the same conception of human nature prevails in both spheres. But does it?

4. If this be nominalism, make the most of it! The interested student will profit by debating whether it is or not (cf. Richard M. Weaver, *Ideas Have Consequences* [Chicago: University of Chicago Press, 1948], pp. 2–9).

There is the point. In practice the two swords do clash. Modern religious thought, in both Protestant and Catholic circles, has gone a very long way toward conceding the moral autonomy of the state as a part of the natural order. But on this road there comes a point beyond which religious teaching ceases to have any relevance at all to temporal affairs, and that is the point to which secular statism is deliberately and systematically pushing the religious institutions. At this point the ultimate challenge arises: What is your conception of the true nature of man? The more concessions one makes to an opposed conception in the initial stages, the tougher is the challenge in the end—as both sides have now discovered. From Germany to Japan the issue now confronts us in quite tangible terms. It is a perennial issue, and there is no reason to suppose that America can evade it. Here again, while no final solution can be argued, I would suggest that the historic study of church-state relations is one of the best preparations for modern citizenship that a serious student can pursue.

3. A more immediate objection to my thesis is advanced by that loyal and caustic commentator, Lawrence Dennis. Dennis has repeatedly argued[5] that when the state sets itself up on a plane of high morality, compromise is very difficult; whereas if it humbly accepts the role of "honest broker," trading and bargaining are more feasible, and peace may be preserved. Dennis refers mainly to international politics, especially to the Wilson-Roosevelt brand of idealism. His observation is realistic and well founded. But it conceals a major moral premise; namely, that peace is preferable to war, even when (as always) a price has to be paid for it; because at least it keeps open the door to future co-operation. How good a bet that is obviously

5. E.g., in his book *The Dynamics of War and Revolution* (New York: Weekly Foreign Letter, 1940), chap. xiii. On the main issue see Winston Churchill's admission of his misgivings regarding the Roosevelt demand for unconditional surrender and the subsequent imposition of the Morgenthau Plan (House of Commons Debates for July 21, 1949; excerpts in American press of July 22).

depends on the validity of the considerations above noted.

The autonomy of these modern nation-states creates problems enough even when it is confined to matters of economics, finance, and currency. When it aspires to morality backed by coercion the situation becomes almost hopeless; but the real problem is not the moral aspiration but the moral autonomy. Hence if morality is to be the criterion of policy, we are compelled to seek principles that are more than merely local or racial. And if we are to preserve "free government or the blessing of liberty," those principles must have a high degree of self-evidence to free people everywhere; for morality, by definition, is bound up with freedom.

In thus pointing out the difficulties of my thesis, I wish to demonstrate the importance of those lines of thought that deal with these perennial problems. Despite the prevailing tendencies of American education, there was never a time when the traditional themes of jurisprudence and moral philosophy were more relevant than now. Just as those themes reasserted themselves in the eighteenth-century crisis, so their study is essential to the far graver crisis of today.

III

THE EXPERIENCE OF CRISIS

☼

EVERY three or four generations, since at least the thirteenth century, the English people have staged a grand dispute as to the terms on which they would obey, or continue to obey, a common political authority. Down to the middle of the seventeenth century in England, to the middle of the nineteenth in America (and later still in Europe), such disputes have involved a considerable amount of bloodshed. It would be optimistic to conclude that that stage is finally over. In any case the argument continues.

Traditionally it takes the form of a debate about the nature of the political community, cast in terms of sovereign and subject, or authority and obedience. The very fact that this dichotomy asserts itself indicates that the basis of community has from time to time actually broken down, inasmuch as mere subjection or obedience constitutes no enduring foundation for an adult common life. It is worth noting, for example, that the sort of creatures upon whom Hobbes lays the duty of obedience with such a heavy hand can hardly be considered adults. These "murderous anarchs" could never in fact have made or maintained the sort of compact that the genial philosopher imputes to them. His emphasis merely reflects the paramount nature of the need for order. That need has led many people to maintain that any order is better than none and compelled many good men to tolerate a degree of tyranny which they profoundly disapproved. Those who have had recent experience of areas in which there is no civil authority, or a conflict of civil authorities, will recognize the force of Hobbes's original position. For practical reasons we are bound to agree on the principle that there must be one and not more than one central repository of the power of coercion. Until that requirement is met, on whatever terms and by whatever means, there can be no security and little economic development. To that extent Hobbes was right in casting the debate about community in terms of sovereignty.

Nonetheless, no final solution can be given merely in terms of the right to coerce. When Treitschke says, "The state is in the first instance power," he is wrong by one figure. The state may be in the second instance power, but in the first instance it is authority; and that authority can never be secure so long as it rests merely on a monopoly of the power to coerce. A brave and brilliant modern scholar—Don Luigi Sturzo—points out that the very nature of man demands that authority be legitimatized, the source of that demand being always the preservation of personal liberty.[1] The necessity of authority, he points out, is not incompatible with the existence of liberty; quite the contrary. But, unless a rational and acceptable *basis* for authority can be maintained, we are landed in the position, with Rousseau no less than Hobbes, that the state is the source of its own authority. Sovereignty then becomes "heteronomous," external to the human personality. It is interesting to notice that Don Sturzo interprets the famous dictum of Paul that "all power is of God" as meaning not a particular sanction of particular authority but that the principle of order itself has a divine basis as applying to human society no less than to the material universe.

We have then two historic foundations for the state: (1) the practical necessity of establishing a monopoly of physical coercion and (2) the rational necessity of legitimizing authority. When circumstances bring these two requirements into

1. *Inner Laws of Society* (New York: P. J. Kenedy, 1944), chap. viii.

conflict, it is the second that in the long run has always proved paramount. We do not, should not, and in the last resort we cannot accede to an unconditional political obedience merely because it is more convenient or comfortable to do so. Even Hobbes gives his poor creatures the right to refuse under certain circumstances—if they can—and strangely enough, one of the grounds he permits them is military conscription.[2]

Our reason for conferring upon the state a monopoly of physical coercion is that by that means we eliminate coercion among ourselves. If private individuals or groups resort to it, we call out the state police to remind them that their mode of procedure constitutes a public nuisance; but this does not mean that we thereby empower the state to settle all the issues that may be in dispute. We do not confer upon the state the exclusive right to define our common ends or a monopoly of means to achieve them. Many civil constitutions, like those of America, set down firmly certain a priori ends with the express intent of limiting the power of the state to monkey about with them. You will recall Lord Acton's praise for the framers of the United States Constitution in that they not only laid down limits on the potency of the State of England but imposed similar limits on the state they were themselves creating. This was merely a special case of the entire tradition of Christianity, interpreted through the great school of natural law. For it is the essence of the Christian position that there are limits both extensive and intensive to the scope and exercise of secular authority. I do not need to remind the reader of the history of this issue; but I do need to emphasize the fact that it is a uniquely Christian tradition and that, whenever and wherever it is denied, the community ceases in both theory and practice to be Christian. Its values as well as its policies undergo a radical change.

2. *Leviathan*, Book II, chap. 21.

I am well aware of a certain embarrassment that arises when one applies the term "Christian" to the thesis that the authority of the state is limited by the rights of free personality. But the time has come when we must look this situation squarely in the face. The feeling of embarrassment arises, in the first place, from the simple fact that most of us are not Christian in any very significant or specific sense. We do, most of us—not all—subscribe to the precepts of Christian morality in a general way; but we do not care to be pressed very far as to the grounds on which they rest. We like to think that decent people of all faiths naturally agree, for example, with the bill of human rights that our delegates urged upon the Assembly of the United Nations; and we are puzzled and affronted when we discover that very large numbers of people, and their delegates, do not agree with our assumptions. It shocks us to realize that vigorous and dynamic social systems can be based on quite different, non-Christian, assumptions—assumptions that practically deify the state. Ostensibly that difference has led, and may again lead, to war. It is therefore advisable that we should be a lot clearer about the basis of our assumptions than, generally speaking, we are.

The contention that the authority of the state is limited by the rights of free personality still rests, for most Americans, on the optimistic view of human nature that was popular in the eighteenth century. That view is neither philosophically nor scientifically adequate to modern needs. The great thinkers and talkers and statesmen of the eighteenth century were riding the crest of the wave. The world was opening up for them, not only geographically but technologically. They could ignore the shadows because they were so sure of a boundless sunrise. It is a marvel that so much of their intellectual achievement is still valid. But we must remember that their century was the bloodiest in modern history—except, of course, our own; that it ended in universal revolution; that its practical legacy was the custom of national war which yet lies like a curse upon us. Their philosophic optimism was a local product. There was little of it left in Europe after 1848.

Its vogue in America was similarly due to circumstances. There is no case in history where so large a tract of this planet, with so favorable a man-land ratio, passed so easily under the control of so intelligent a leadership as that of the United States; and there will never be another. Let us remember that, when we propagate our optimistic universalism. Is it reasonable to suppose that the native inhabitants of Malaya, Indochina, the Dutch East Indies, central Africa, India, Japan, China—many of whom are as intelligent and as highly educated as we are—will accept our eighteenth-century assumptions as placidly as we do? Why should they? Our political philosophy is perhaps less the result of good thinking than of good luck. And as R. G. Hawtrey pointed out some years ago in Boston, under the nation-state system the good luck of one set of people is usually the bad luck of another.

But if we are pushed back beyond the local assumptions of eighteenth-century optimism, we seem to be heading for trouble; and we would rightly avoid it—if we can. I have said that the principle of limiting state authority by the rights of free personality is a specifically Christian principle. I have suggested that the eighteenth-century version of that principle was somewhat local and fortuitous and so continues to be. Our ideal universalism must rest on deeper and wider foundations. But when we attempt to dig down to those foundations we become apprehensive that old ghosts may rise again. There are those among us who are doing their best to revive the old quarrel of church and state. Both Catholics and Calvinists have in times past attempted to dictate policy to the state, even to control it. Organized atheism has made similar attempts, and in some parts of the world it has succeeded. There are practical consequences. In the sphere of values it is simply not possible to be neutral—neither individually nor collectively.

Our tradition—to take what may seem a minor point—calls for courtesy; as we often say, Christian courtesy. It requires that we say in effect to the other fellow, whatever his station, "You are as good as I am." At least in theory we do not allow that statement to be qualified by race, color, or creed. The grounds of that assertion lie much deeper than Rousseau or Tom Paine. Where they are not understood, the statement goes into reverse; it becomes, "I am as good as you are." There is no courtesy, no mutuality in that; the resulting difference in social attitude is immense and increasingly evident. It is the part of wisdom to recognize that what our tradition demands of us in this matter is a more than natural virtue; a quality of conduct that cannot be attained or maintained without training; a high-tension level from which we are always prone to relapse into something much nearer the brute. But if we do relapse, democracy becomes unworkable. We have seen that happen.

Again, our tradition demands of us an extraordinary tolerance of speech and opinion. We know, of course, that any people which suppresses or eliminates its minorities hamstrings its own progress. We have seen that happen. During the recent war there were many good Americans who felt that our—or must one still say, Mr. Justice Holmes's—criterion of "clear and present danger" was not a sufficient safeguard against dissentient opinion; and there was, in fact, more persecution of such opinion than the public was aware of, far more than was practiced in England. But looking over the record, as it begins to appear, it may be held that a little more opposition would not have been a bad thing—had it been permitted. For even on critical occasions we may do the commonweal more harm by excessive suppression than by sticking to toleration.

There is risk either way; the latter is often more obvious, the former more vital.

But it is not on such pragmatic grounds that the tradition of free speech relies. It is asserted in our Constitution as a human right; and the only limitation on it—a tacit limitation at that—is that it is the right of a particular kind of man; namely, an honest man. That is all; but how much! Once again we find our system resting on a certain level of virtue—a level that we do not find everywhere. If the exponents of dissent deem it proper to their creeds to lie or forge or deliberately deceive, we have no option but to declare, on that sole ground, that they render themselves outlaws. Our system cannot contain or co-operate with such people, because, little though we realize it, democracy is a proposition in morality. A very exacting and hazardous proposition.

If this be granted—and much more evidence could be cited—the nature, and the limits, of the state become clearer. A great contemporary scholar points out that the democratic state, whether monarchical or republican, must have real power to command.[3] If free men deny this, they cut the ground from under their own feet. But the monopoly of coercion that we give to the state does not convey a monopoly of valuations. That is the great temptation of democracy. We are urged to suppose that because the procedures are democratic—or can be made to pass as such—therefore the state acquires an unlimited competence in the definition and formulation of the *ends* of collective and personal life. As soon as that assumption is accepted (or "put over"), the democratic means may themselves be discarded, and our entire fate then passes into the hands of an uncontrolled and irresponsible executive. We have seen that happen. In a true democracy the criteria and the ends of collective action must at all times be evident and acceptable to you and me, because they are the values of personality. That

3. Pope Pius XII, Christmas message, 1944.

was what the founders of this country assumed when they held certain truths to be self-evident. That is what we assume when we extol what we call "Americanism." Whatever may be true of other states, the values of American patriotism are universal moral values; whenever and wherever they cease to be such, our democracy becomes just another bubble on the bloody stream of time.

The "American way of life" admits of no precise definition, and the phrase has been exploited *ad nauseam*. But one meaning can be attributed to it with some certainty: it connotes a rough, tough, social synthesis that can absorb and utilize more of the dynamic abilities of free individuals than any other system in history. Some of the results, and some of the individuals, were, and are, exceedingly rough and tough. But the American way was to take a chance on humanity, treat the freaks and the failures as mere aberrations from a norm of natural decency, and avoid general coercion like the plague. When all the scores are in, all shortcomings and defections duly noted, the net result has been an astounding success. It stands unequaled and unchallenged by any other system on earth.

Take the most obvious and therefore least-noted feature. The United States has produced by far the finest breed of human animals the planet has ever seen. They are bigger, stronger, longer-lived (Sweden and New Zealand come closest). They have better bodies, better feet, better teeth, and a glorious proportion of sheer physical beauty. Every dawn over America should be greeted with a "Te Deum laudamus." There is a vague and widespread impression that most of this is due to good luck. Not so. It is true that the man-land ratio in North America, for the last two centuries, has been favorable by old-economy standards (it can be too low as well as too high). But the natural resources of the area are not exceptional. The European peninsula is in essentials more richly endowed.[4] It is the human factor that counts. Human beings of all sorts and backgrounds were given a new chance in the New World to try out a new freedom on a new scale which in the Old World was thwarted by the historic ossifications. They tried it, and by and large they succeeded. Their present worries and embarrassments arise, to a far greater degree than they know, from their reinvolvement in the dead-end parochialisms of the Old World. To take a single instance: could anything be more fantastic on the record than the idea that Americans as such should go to school to Moscow? That individual Americans (or English or French or any other sort) may learn much from individual Russians (or Chinese or Japanese or Hindus or any other sort) is so much testimony to the universality of truth and value. But the notion that the American way of life as such could be improved by an injection of traditional Slavic despotism is plausible only to people who misunderstand, or have never seriously considered, the foundations of the American way.

Just because it is the way of freedom, there is a disposition to assume that it has no particular rules, postulates, ethics, or fundamental principles. People will tell you that "it makes no difference what a man believes so long as, etc." It makes all the difference in the world. On the practical plane, a man who believes in the worth-whileness of his job and the essential fairness of the economic system that controls him is likely to average a better and happier day's work than a man who resents the whole business. But there is far more to it than that. The history of modern Germany, Austria, France, Russia, Spain, Italy, Ireland, and even England shows what can happen to any community whose spiritual or ideological solidarity begins to crack. Usually, as the critical stage comes on,

4. See the detailed and very significant comparison in Barbara Ward's recent book *The West at Bay* (New York: W. W. Norton Co., 1948), p. 77.

some group emerges that tries to hold the society together by sheer force. This is the familiar phase of the "man on horseback." Perfervid nationalism is its banner: solidarity for solidarity's sake. This phase never lasts. Sometimes its policies collide with those of similar groups abroad; always they are challenged by less atavistic groups at home. From one collision or the other (sometimes both) arises the catastrophic phase of crisis. Its signal is a universal apprehension, like that aroused by the approach of a hurricane. People know that, short of a miracle, the sequel is likely to be ruinous, bloody, and prolonged. They fear far more than they hope. There is talk of the end of an era, the collapse of civilization. There is also a general feeling of impotence. People do not see what more they can do, what more they could have done, to avert what looks like doom. This is not surprising, since the whole situation arises from an inability to comprehend, and therefore to respond to, the challenge of change in the first place.

Change comes anyway; the challenge is to determine whether it shall follow the pattern of growth or of dissolution. That is a real choice, a real challenge. One has to state categorically that the issue is not predetermined, never a foregone conclusion. It is simply not permissible to hold that the choice is illusory, powerful as the temptation may be. The temptation is part of the challenge. Such a belief, like any other faith, is an act of will; and in social fatalism the will is to suicide. It denies the humanity of humanity, turns the creature against himself in a mood corresponding to the perversion of the generative function, which is one of its most widespread symptoms. Spenglerian epics, Wagnerian fourth acts, existential melodramas, are all very well as playthings of the mind, stimuli to the imagination; but, taken seriously, they play themselves out in dying bodies, dying souls, and dying nations.

Change comes anyway and many ways. The factors that

demand it have a knack of piling up, like those of the business cycle. The intellectual life of mankind does not stand still—how could it?—but it does not follow a straight course either. At one time pure speculation is dominant, at another contrivance or politics or the arts. These are not haphazard variations; if they were, they would be meaningless, severally or in succession. Each phase is in some degree prompted by circumstances, and each bequeaths something to posterity—something of truth and, as a rule, something of error. Thus the prompting circumstances are never wholly material or wholly contemporary. The same environment that urges change conveys strong elements of continuity, of inertia; this is the typical crisis structure.

"Environment" is a clumsy term here; some people prefer "culture." Either will serve provided we realize that the reference is not merely to something "out there"—like the flora and fauna of a particular geographical or social or academic situation—but to something "in here," inside what we call ourselves. For present purposes we may ignore the philosophic problems raised by this distinction if we recall how often people say, apropos some question of politics or principle, that they feel "torn two ways"; or if we note the current high proportion of schizophrenics—sure sign of the depth of our crisis. The amazing sales of Rabbi Liebman's book *Peace of Mind*, and of less meritorious works offering psychological panaceas of one sort or another, show the extent to which the crisis is felt as personal, not merely environmental. Every great turning point in history has documented the subjective aspect; that is indeed the principal symptom of a major crisis.

In the external aspect this piling-up of the factors making for change is often called the "cultural lag." That very useful concept refers to the fact that once in a while some particular phase of human activity rushes ahead at a pace with which other phases simply cannot keep up. In our time, of course, the obvious example is the speed of technological advance as compared with the inertia of traditional behavior patterns and social institutions. The contrast is blazoned on the front page of every newspaper. We are forced to recognize that applied science, for better or worse, has at last made possible the ideal of planetary community.[5] And what a community it might be: how fertile, how rich in every sense, how varied and joyful! The prophets have always dreamed of it. At the same time we have to wade through acres of swampland in which old patterns of tribal patriotism, limited self-interest, and local security exhale an atmosphere of decadence and despair. Everyone politely pretends to ignore the smell; and everyone knows where it comes from. If only our minds could acquire the wings that our machines have taken!

Yet there is something to be said for inertia. Without it the entire physical universe would fly apart in centrifugal incoherence; and something of the sort may be true of the social and psychological universe of modern man. It does not follow that, because the cultural lag is a fact, everything ought to be geared up to the speed of applied science. There are phases of human achievement more important than flying machines or washing machines that will not tolerate any such acceleration. Consider, for example, the effect of the current technological revolution on family life, on the family as an institution. There is a problem here about which many good books, especially novels, have been written; but none of them can be said to have solved it. What an agony German and Russian parents have had with it in our time! Most American parents also are up against it, at least in some of its practical aspects; as a rule, it has them licked. Perhaps it would help if more of the children could be brought to consider it with them.

Similarly, the bonds—both personal and institutional—that

5. Also, of course, planetary destruction.

hold society together on the larger scale are undergoing a terrific strain; and some of them are cracking under it. The traditional legal concepts of equity, fairness, property, competition, public interest; the traditional political concepts of nationality, sovereignty, democracy, equality, self-determination—all these, and many more, are feeling the impact of what applied science has done to society, group life, domestic and international relations. And now is the day of reckoning. The factors of change are piled up to a head that may at any time, and any one of a dozen places, burst the remaining bounds of the established order.

The power of these factors is curiously recognized in Anglo-American foreign policy. The rise of modern Germany, and its disturbing impact on the world since 1870, are inseparable from its amazing technological progress. We are therefore deliberately destroying the results, and to a large degree the foundations, of that progress in the interests of a hypothetical security; while at the same time we stake immense quantities of our goods and resources on the reconstruction of a Europe stripped of its dynamic center. Similarly, we apply economic blockade and boycott to the Slavic system in the same hope of containing the disturbance created by another area of rapidly changing culture; its rulers reply in kind. Inevitably our policies seem to take on a merely status quo-ish character in Russian eyes; theirs a merely aggressive character in ours. Neither aspect depicts the whole truth. There is no denying the fact of conflict or the possibility of disaster. Where will and intelligence have so far failed is in the invention of broader and higher types of synthesis, within which problems of mutual adjustment, however difficult and prolonged, need not issue in mass murder. Thus the situation presents itself as a life-and-death struggle of mere "powers" over a limited total of land and "resources." Yet every instructed person knows that that pattern is not imposed upon us by external circumstances. It is not an objective picture. It is simply the reflection of the present limits of will and intelligence. Every concession made, every condition accepted, for the sake of a larger synthesis, could be rewarded a hundred fold in the ultimate fruition of world community. It is highly speculative to invest in the future of humanity. But, if one refuses, is any other investment safer?

We must beware of assuming that all the elements of the current crisis, or the "cultural lag," derive directly or indirectly from the technological change. Most people do assume that, even when they deny the assumption; for it is only a minority that now accords a real autonomy to the intellectual or spiritual life of man. Even in religious thought, the thesis that the life of humanity is determined by its material circumstances has made subtle and profound headway. Nearly all schools, however, would agree that it is the uneven technological advance which has given the cutting edge to the cultural conflict. Without that factor, there would still be conflict, or, at least, contention; but nowadays it would probably stop short of the killing stage. While there is still plenty of talk about crusades and ideologies, it is doubtful whether recent wars have been, or whether future wars will be, fought on purely ideal grounds; and it is significant that neither the Vatican nor the League of Nations ever sanctioned war on that basis. True, both Wilson and Roosevelt II based their early approaches to a war policy on moralistic arguments, but in their final triumphs over the opposition the appeal was to more tangible considerations of American interest and security. Thus the technological factor remains the critical one in the international as well as in the domestic situation. It is from that quarter that the most urgent challenge comes.

Now whatever curbs we may see fit to impose on conquered Germany and Japan, or obstreperous Russia, or any other trouble spots in this respect, we are not likely to impose any on ourselves. Historians may remember that, when England sought to trim the economic life of America to fit her mercantile plan, she also put reciprocal restraints upon English enterprise. They were not very painful; even if they had been, the plan would scarcely have won more conformity from the colonists. But, at least, the principle was recognized. Who would dream today of putting restraints on American enterprise in the interests of a wider plan? The mere charge of attempting it is enough to get an indictment from any grand jury against any American corporation. We are all for free competition so long as we feel sure we can win. No matter how far "with pitfall and with gin" a benevolent government besets the path of free enterprise, who wants to forego its achievements? Who would dream of telling American enterprisers to stop enterprising, American inventors to stop inventing, American investors to stop investing (one wishes they would only begin again, and Mr. Eric Johnston currently proposes that the government underwrite them!). One used to say in Europe that the solvency of America depends upon the speed of obsolescence. Who wants to stop it? Even the professional enemies of free enterprise show no conspicuous desire to forego its benefits. They spend their hard-earned incomes on its new materials, new gadgets and techniques, new time- and life- and effort-savers, just like the rest of us; nor have they convinced themselves or anybody else that unfree enterprise has done or could do better. What then?

If we in America intend (as apparently we do) to continue staking our fortune on the voluntary system, we should realize, and make sure that our children realize, what we are doing. That system has faults, like any other system; and in difficult times the faults get much more attention than the benefits. Public opinion seems to hold that the faults, grave as they are, are not so bad on the whole as those of the coercive systems; but it is nonetheless disposed to sanction large doses of coercion (under the label "regulation") partly in a genuine desire for the improvement of the voluntary system, but also with the intention of forcing more out of it for this or that particular pressure group than it is presently giving—despite the admitted fact that it is now giving more than any system known to history. Perhaps both aims can be realized without the collapse of the system. But care and caution are needed lest the final verdict be that of the old medical story—"operation successful, patient unfortunately died."

That is one phase of the situation which we shall examine in some detail. But underlying it, and governing all major decisions, is the more general question we have been discussing. If we accept the dynamism of the voluntary system, and its technological drive, as axiomatic, we thereby accept the challenge it offers to the survival of those mental, emotional, and institutional patterns by which our personal and social lives have so largely been shaped. There are deep-rooted habits, associations, values, as to which young people of today feel "torn two ways," whose survival really is threatened, whose disappearance would leave a real void, a deep spiritual insecurity. Perhaps it is foolish even to discuss this phase of the crisis; but it was precisely such a void, such an insecurity, that gave fascism and naziism and communism their unique opportunity. We may have thwarted their immediate effects. Have we anything with which to counter their disturbing idealism?

Few informed persons would give a prompt and unqualified affirmative. Most would probably say, "Well, we could have, or we should have, if—or but—." To speak frankly, much of the current praise of free enterprise falls rather flat upon the modern ear. It is an old song by this time (the younger generation has the adjective "corny"), and there are not so many voices eager to swell the old refrain—perhaps for just that reason. It no longer sounds revolutionary or adventurous, as it did in the eighteenth century; and young people of all ages crave a cause with a kick in it, something they can take a risk for and even (up to a point) suffer for. Many American good causes owe more to this craving than to the merits of the case.

Then the very success of the voluntary system in the production and distribution of goods (granted that it is far from perfect, especially in the latter function) evokes the accusation of materialism. German philosophers were making that charge against the school of Adam Smith almost before he was dead; they have never ceased, and the charge has had a widespread modern revival. It gets its force not so much from the deficiencies of original liberalism as from the fact that freedom itself, as it is increasingly attained, loses its appeal if we persistently refuse to ask, or fail to define, what freedom is for.

Many people are tempted, in the very name of freedom, to deny any such obligation. Their position is to be respected. But around it all the weaknesses of individualism make their last stand. For what actually emerges is not a pleasant symphony of suspended judgments but a clashing confusion of purposes and ideals whose only common cry is for goods, goods, and more goods—which satisfies nobody's aspirations. This is the stage at which materialism takes possession as it were by default, without any legitimate title; and a society abounding in good works as well as good intentions stands baffled and bewildered before its supreme opportunity.

In collective as well as personal life, we sometimes need to look back to learn how to go forward. It is well from time to time to refresh our sense of direction by reviewing the way we have traveled. When our forefathers advised "a frequent recurrence to fundamental principles," they knew what they were talking about. Principles that are really fundamental do not go out of date. They are modes of truth in action and, as such, partake of that dynamic quality which we find in every gospel image of truth. They are therefore always rewardful to study, always fruitful under cultivation. Take this of Jefferson, for example: "The God who gave us life gave us liberty at the same time; the hand of force may destroy, but cannot disjoin them." That statement, says his principal biographer, "belongs, not to the American colonies, but to mankind; not to the year 1774 merely, but to all the years thereafter."[6] Well said, indeed; for surely, if the statement has lost its meaning, then America exists no longer. Yet every term and every concept in it now calls for fresh defining.

These evocative statements of the eighteenth-century revolution are all like that; and we shall not begin to grasp their significance until we recognize that *they are acts of will, not merely of intellect*. The intuition governs the logic, because what is affirmed goes far beyond what can be strictly proved. Decisive moments in history always produce such affirmations—which are actions rather than propositions—simply because it becomes necessary to "make up one's mind." And making up one's mind involves certain deliberate, often hazardous, choices in the sphere of values.

Much of the sterility of modern social philosophy arises from its tendency to represent life by a well-integrated set of concepts, with the values and purposes stuck in afterward like decorated skewers or Christmas candles. No philosophy that pulls human nature to pieces in that fashion will have much effect on human action. We refute it after the manner of Dr. Johnson. True, we test our immediate purposes by our values, or, if we do not, history will do it for us; but we do not deduce our values from our concepts. They come from somewhere else; they rest on an original act of affirmation or intuition, as does the United States of America—"We hold these truths to be self-evident." Every sound philosophy, from Aristotle on,

6. D. Malone, *Jefferson the Virginian* (Boston: Little, Brown & Co., 1948), p. 188.

starts with an affirmation which is an act of will. It says, "The nature of man is thus and so, and *therefore*. . . ." The beginning of wisdom is to recognize the character, the locus, of this affirmation.

For when we say that the origin of every effective social philosophy is an act of affirmation, which is an act of will, we do not mean that the act is arbitrary. As to the content of the affirmation, we have apparently a wide choice: we may affirm the libidinous man of Dr. Freud, or the biological man of Herbert Spencer and Mussolini, or the racial man of Gobineau and his followers, or the "murderous anarch" of Thomas Hobbes, Esq., or the hedonistic man of the utilitarians who knew so pathetically little about pleasure, or the economic man of my tough North Country ancestors, or the rational man who rang the "Angelus" of the Goddess of Reason with the rope of the guillotine, or any of the current varieties of Marxist man, or even the poor old *Homo sapiens* of H. G. Wells. But none of these choices is arbitrary. Each of them represents a certain disposition, or predisposition, of the mind, acting within a given set of circumstances, in a situation that compels consciousness of alternatives. Then, as we say, people have to "argue it out with themselves"—have not thousands of our contemporaries had that experience? It is the main theme of modern literature.

The argument is often prolonged and painful; theory will seem to pull one way, lifelong associations another, an inbred or innate sense of values a third. This personal experience of crisis can reach the point of agony and the verge of madness.[7] Let us take heart and be strong in it, precisely because its urgency is *not* an illusion, its significance *not* merely subjective.[8] This is truly the point at which the historic environ-

7. See, e.g., *The Journals of André Gide* (New York: A. A. Knopf, 1947), Vol. II (years 1916–17). Scores of such references could be cited.

8. For further on this see my book *The Liberal Tradition* (New Haven: Yale University Press, 1945), chap. xi, esp. pp. 210–13.

ment, or culture, is alive and working out its destiny. Apart from the individual life-experience, the culture is something read about in books, absorbed from the radio, studied in schools, museums, movie houses, and indoctrination courses, canned for export and sold in packages at home. Whatever life there is in it lives in and through the living person, meets in his consciousness the wrestling angel, wins from his tenacity alone the knowledge of its weakness and the chance of another dawn.

IV

THE MORAL BASIS OF THE STATE

☼

SO FAR my argument has been that the unique attribute of the modern state is the power of legitimized coercion. We give it that in order to get rid of miscellaneous coercion among ourselves, which is another name for chaos. That was Hobbes's main point, and a good one. But in our tradition coercion is *ipso facto* something to be held to a minimum, because we set store on the development of free self-governing personalities. So we can hope for order and stability only if the fundamental principles on which our community is based are such as to enlist the voluntary allegiance of free people.

Historically, they were such. They were affirmations, acts of will, that went beyond any particular economic or political theory. Their theory is now somewhat dated and needs restating;[1] but the affirmations stand if we are still agreed as to the values they embodied. Are we still agreed? Do critics of the theory also challenge the values?

Not, as a rule, directly. But life, liberty, and the pursuit of happiness do acquire a different aspect under modern nationalism and industrialization. New problems arise, traditional values get pushed around, and to many people new norms of conduct are at least suggested. For example, the value of honesty in public life and utterance has taken a bad beating in—or rather, by—our generation; not to mention courtesy and tolerance. Circumstances, no doubt, alter cases; the question is how much else they alter. We are not talking about

1. On this see the excellent study by J. H. Hallowell, *The Decline of Liberalism as an Ideology* (Berkeley: University of California Press, 1943).

deviations from accepted norms, of which there are always plenty; we are talking about actual denial or rejection of the norms, tacit or avowed, of which there is now a significant amount. I would venture to say that this rejection is producing, in certain geographical and ideational areas, a recognizable type of personality alien to American tradition. When your values change, you change.

Moreover, there is a whole class of problems stemming straight out of our conception of freedom. Freedom of natural persons has been interpreted, almost from the start of this republic, to include freedom to form voluntary associations for any purposes not declared illegitimate. Is that right—it is generally held to be such—still valid? Is it absolute? If not, what restraints or limiting assumptions apply? Such questions cannot be settled merely on a basis of whether, or how much, this or that group of people feels discommoded by the application of the principle. That is the way in which popular politics does in fact tend to approach the problem; but the vacillations of our courts as well as legislatures are enough to show that it is not an adequate way. We have to dig deeper, to re-examine our "fundamental principles," to take a closer look at the foundations of our type of state as compared with those of other types.

We may, I think, begin with a short cut that will save us a lot of what used to be very tough going: we may take it for granted that any modern state is based on law, not mere personal fiat. To those who know only the polemical version of the nature and activities of the authoritarian states this may seem a surprising assertion; but there is the solid fact that these states, especially Nazi Germany and Soviet Russia, have gone to tremendous pains and produced literally tons of literature to establish precisely this point about their own systems. Moreover, the comic-strip version of history, which ascribes all the trouble to the Big Bad Man, is at least as well known to the leaders of such states as it is to us; and so is its silly suggestion that, once the villain is disposed of, everybody will think and behave just as we do, and all will be well. No, the problem lies on a much deeper level than that; it raises the question of what we (and they) understand by law and the foundations of law.

Here again we may take a short cut through what is really a semantic jungle. Jurists have the old Austinian maxim that law is what the courts will enforce; the legislature is supposed to define it, but, once defined, there it is. Against this may be set the opposing maxim, conspicuous in America since the years of prohibition but actually much older: law is what the citizens will obey. Most of this difficulty arises from the ambiguity, in English, of the word "law." In the one case we are talking about the rules and practice of coercion; in the other we are talking about *Recht* or *jus*—that is, about the *reasons why* people submit to rules and allow themselves to be coerced.[2] The ambiguity is so striking, and to foreign jurists so exasperating, that it suggests a definite bias: as if British thought did not want the distinction to be too sharp. This is perhaps confirmed by the great importance of equity in the British tradition.

However that may be, any people to whom personal freedom is a cardinal value will not tolerate an absolute distinction between positive or enunciated law—lawyers' law—and the basic principles of obligation which we may perhaps call philosophers' law. The average person, though certainly not a lawyer or a lover of lawyers, has a native propensity to philosophize; American lore and literature bear witness to that. It is a factor to be encouraged and utilized.

2. A useful American reference is J. C. Gray, *The Nature and Sources of the Law* (New York: Columbia University Press, 1909), chap. xiii. Gray's attitude to natural law is interesting; at one point he calls it "this exploded superstition" and immediately readmits it with a different label.

In jurisprudence we are concerned mainly with the sources of law, historical as well as philosophical. This study is especially important to a republic, whether it be ancient Rome or modern America. Gray,[3] among others, argues that the notion of sovereignty is an unnecessary nuisance, and I am inclined to agree with him; for a general understanding and consensus as to the sources of law will render the Austinian concept superfluous, in practice as well as theory. The important question is whether such a consensus exists. I doubt whether it does, now in America; witness the remarkable increase in split decisions and hotly contested opinions of the Supreme Court, to say nothing of lower courts and legislatures. Of course, there must and should be specific differences of opinion at all levels; but in a stable society there also must and should be a general consensus as to fundamental principles. The lack of that—still more, its deliberate destruction—would be a matter of the gravest public concern.[4]

But how is it to be strengthened or restored? Obviously not by force. This is one of the vital areas where even "force to the uttermost" will not settle the issue—thank goodness! Free and fair debate, backed by honest good will, is all we have to rely on. But the consensus, the necessary minimum area of assent, must express the integral personality of civilized man, not just his rather limited "rational" or economic calculations. Since this is where my thesis differs from other well-argued and popular views, I may clarify it by contrast with an excellent statement of another position.

Dr. Hans Meyerhoff, in a recent study of "The Social Philosophies of Our Time,"[5] reviews the four leading types and frankly states that the democratic doctrine, stemming from

3. *Ibid.*, chap. iii.

4. Only after this passage was written did I receive the book by Wilhelm Röpke, *Civitas humana* (Eng. trans.; London, 1948). Even more than the previous work of the distinguished author, it abounds in original observations on this point.

5. *American Perspective*, III, No. 3 (June, 1949), 136–53.

the school of Locke, Montesquieu, and Jefferson, "failed to provide a satisfactory frame of reference for the radical material and intellectual transformations our society has undergone during the last century, and this failure has been generally admitted." The author recognizes that the failure is not merely pragmatic, but involves the maintenance and definition of values. We quarrel not only about ways and means but also about ends. Looking at the facts with a detachment that is rare in this sort of argument, Dr. Meyerhoff says:

> The various theories, reviewed above, differ, as we have seen, in their interpretation of these values as much from each other as from the democratic concepts. However, if we assume—as we must unless we admit intellectual defeat—that there is some way of settling these differences, the method by which we determine the meaning of these values and the criteria by which we test their claim to validity are of crucial importance. Thus the differences in the contents of social philosophies are inseparable from differences in method.
>
> The method of the democratic tradition consists essentially in recognizing the rational criteria of argument and proof developed by the natural sciences as the only authority for judging the validity of a social theory. It follows that, however damaging the original impact of the social sciences has been on the traditional body of beliefs and values, a reconstruction of this tradition is possible only through the best possible use of the techniques developed and results obtained by these sciences.
>
> From this point of view, social philosophy is simply the sum total of the methods and theories developed by biology, psychology, anthropology, sociology, economics and political science. . . .

Now any teacher or writer with experience in this field will at once protest that there is no "sum total." These methods and theories simply do not add up. They scatter.[6] But Meyer-

6. This is not, of course, to deny that there are plenty of synthetic philosophies; the names of Comte, Spencer, Wells, and perhaps Dewey spring at once to mind. But the point is that these are all personal constructs with which other persons may disagree. Is an aggregative approach more feasible or more promising? The issue was clearly stated by President Burkhardt of Bennington College in his inaugural address in 1947:

hoff admits this: "The method borrowed from the natural sciences has so far failed to clarify the status of value judgments which occupy a dominant place in the social sciences." Nonetheless, he argues, what else can you do? The scientific method is intrinsically self-critical and therefore provides for a constant revision of its own conclusions; and, further,

it recognizes only *rational* criteria of evidence and proof as legitimate authority for establishing and enforcing conclusions affecting the social behavior. For this reason, it has consistently rejected any other type of "authority"—whether divine right, irrational myths or absolute truths—as illegitimate for the construction of a social order. It is not claimed that other criteria may not be significant for other aspects of human experience (the arts or religion, for example); it is maintained only that, insofar as man's social organization is concerned, no arguments and propositions other than those which can stand the test of rational inquiry be admitted as final arbiters of what is true and false or right and wrong. Thus the coercion of men for the purpose of constructing or preserving a social order can be justified only if and when men everywhere, regardless of creed, color and social position, consent freely because the social system proceeds from principles which can be tested and defended on the grounds of rational argument. Freedom, therefore, is assumed to consist (*a*) in the recognition of (and, hence, submission to) these principles on the basis of no other authority than the individual's own rational powers and (*b*) in the creation of a social order providing the optimum conditions for the development of these and other potentialities of the individual. . . .

With the second proviso the present writer, like all liberals, is heartily in agreement. But does the authority of "the individual's own rational powers" actually constitute a sufficient

---

"Education today must provide a Science of Man which is commensurate with our knowledge and control of nature. . . . One group believes that the Science of Man is already complete, that it is stored up in the accumulated wisdom of the past. . . . The other group believes that the Science of Man has only begun to be worked, that it will come only as a result of the application of scientific methods of research to our social problems."

basis for the voluntary consensus that underlies every free society? Both historically and philosophically there is room for doubt, not of the logic but of the conception of "the individual" that is tacitly assumed. It is here that the atomistic assumption of the French revolutionaries so subtly enters in; and it is here that the superficial logic of their tradition deceives the individual as to his own reality, his own significance, his place in history and society. He knows better, but he has lost the power to argue his own case.

If the individual's own "rational powers" are all we have to rely on in the construction of a true community, we shall hardly escape the brand of materialism that makes a true community impossible. We shall find ourselves saying, as the laissez faire theorists did, that after all, he knows his own business better than anyone else; and we may miss the question, of which the ordinary person is at least sometimes aware, whether his own business is all that he needs to know. Not, of course, that we expect him to be fidgeting and worrying all the time about the social significance of his various doings and transactions. He has to make a living and bring up a family, and as a rule that is quite enough to worry about. The point at issue is the conception of the individual that underlies the theory of democracy; and I am suggesting that the "rationalistic" conception is too narrow and shallow to constitute a sound point of departure. Spawned by modern scientism on modern industrialism,[7] it has acquired a specious plausibility,

7. Cf. the following from Röpke (*op. cit.*, p. 140): "Life consists in the short rhythm of the weekly pay-day. It is an existence which has been torn from its firm anchorage, namely, property, the warmth of community, natural surroundings and the family. At the same time, work instead of being a satisfaction and fulfilment of life becomes a mere means, and the hours spent at work a mere liability, whereas these ought to represent an asset in the balance-sheet of life. Compensation is sought all the more eagerly in consumption, but more often than not this means pleasures and distractions which are no less mechanical than the work. This floating humanity, the modern nomads . . ." contains, I suspect, a good many American veterans. Some of them may be willing to wrestle with the difficult questions (and the difficult English) in a common effort to find a practical answer.

especially in academic circles; but even at its best it is incomplete, unrealistic, and needs making over into something more like a human being. For this reason it is not only unsound as a postulate but illegitimate even as an ideal.

This line of criticism makes some ultra-rationalists very angry.[8] They are so sure of the way people ought to act that they resent not only the counterargument (it is not the way people ought to act) but the counterassertion (it is not the way people do act). Some of them have indulged in a degree of violence that is historically remarkable. Even in normally respectable quarters, where serious and responsible writing is to be expected, reviews of anti-statist literature are now frequently mere tirades, not above personal abuse and deliberate misrepresentation. There is enough material to sustain a good doctoral thesis on the nature of the controversy. The amount of passion let loose on both sides suggests that we are getting down to issues that are psychologically deeper than most of us realize. That is one of the really encouraging aspects of the situation. But, for the same reason, one has to be especially careful to make the right distinctions; and in what I have written above there is a distinction involved that a quick reader will certainly miss and a hostile one distort. Here it is:

If we argue that the rationalistic conception of human nature is inadequate as a basis for social or political community, are we not thereby opening the door to a totalitarian conception? Is not that precisely what the totalitarian states did? If it is argued that a more total or comprehensive conception of human nature is required as a basis of human community, how is one to escape the charge that such a conception will lead to an unlimited authoritarianism?

The answer is obvious but not easy, because it involves a further challenge. If the basic conception is true, then accordance with the authority that rests upon it will be essentially

8. E.g., Lancelot Hogben, *Retreat from Reason* (Northampton, Mass., 1937).

spontaneous; if it is false, then the accordance will be essentially coercive. Surely we have enough evidence of that. The challenge consists in the simple fact that one has to make up one's mind about the nature of man. This is a difficult job. Some settle it on a hereditary or traditional basis; some (unlucky ones) have to argue it out with themselves; some try to ignore it. But in serious practical politics it cannot finally be ignored.

I said above that every major political system rests on an act of affirmation as to the nature of man. Such acts get embodied in social institutions, which are a sort of continuous affirmation. The state, as one of these, has the unique attribute of legitimized coercion. The affirmation it embodies is therefore by nature moral rather than political or economic. This implies at least the possibility, on the fundamental plane, of absolute truth and error as to the nature of man, and absolute right and wrong in the sphere of morality. It also implies that the alternatives, on that plane, can be certainly known.

This position is close to that of the Dutch jurist, Hugo Krabbe. He depicts the state as a community founded on law, to which he ascribes its sole authority. He maintains, in terms that Cicero would not have disputed, that human will is itself constrained by what he calls the "sense of right" (*Rechtsbewusstsein*), to which he imputes a high degree of objectivity. That is to say, right and wrong are really there, in the nature of things; and, while it may take effort and training fully to know them and apply them, we must not suppose that we invent them or tolerate any theory which suggests, however subtly, that we do.

But here is the difficulty: How are we to be sure that what passes for the sense of right may not be in fact just class interest or national interest (demand for security, etc.)? As we all know, there is a very vocal school of thought that depicts conscience itself as merely a reflection of the environment—social, economic, technological—and therefore determined by local circumstances. In that case, apparently, law as Krabbe describes it can have no final objectivity or universality. But, apart from the circular nature of this argument, it is not sufficiently in accord with the facts. There is much truth in it, but the really cogent truth is overlooked. The exponents of moral relativity seek to impress us with such facts as Spartan infanticide, temple prostitution, Athenian pederasty, Egyptian royal incest, and a varied collection of the taboos of primitive peoples all of which in their time and place presumably functioned as moral criteria. We may admit all these archeological curiosities, and their modern counterparts, into our perspective simply because there is a perspective and we did not invent it.

The controlling historical fact in this matter is the capacity of human beings to give spontaneous recognition and tenacious adherence to higher moral criteria when they are presented, regardless of any current or calculated advantage. This fact may be viewed as an instance of Toynbee's concept of "challenge." It illustrates that mode of behavior of living things that we call "teleological." The difficulty many people have in accepting this term springs from the impossibility of defining, to the complete satisfaction of our limited minds, the end, the *telos*. But this difficulty is really a hangover from the age of dogmatic quantification. If we could ever exhaustively define the *telos*, our human problem would promptly end with a "Q.E.D.," and our story would be over; there would be no earthly reason for adding another line to it. It is significant that all attempts to frame an exhaustive definition—Bentham's, for example—look a little comic to posterity.

But have we not begged the whole question by the introduction into our statement of the word "higher"? Here again our appeal must be to facts (it is striking how recent social and economic theory dislikes that appeal). It is a fact that modern democratic society has reached a stage more favorable to the development of free personality, on the widest possible plane, than any society known to history. If that fact does not justify our use of the term "higher," there is no criterion that will—indeed, there is no criterion whatever. Of course there are all sorts of qualifications and reservations. The mere fact that we are aware of them shows that we know in our bones what we are talking about. In both individual and social life we recognize by common consent the difference of direction between "higher" and "lower." When we fail or fall short, we know it, and we say so. Our ideal is no abstraction. Where in the world will you find more kitchens and living-rooms, more classrooms and assemblies, in which people of strongly opposed convictions can speak from the heart without mutual fear? It is not merely in the formation of opinion but in the education of personality that such places fulfil their social function; and when they are threatened, from whatever quarter, we instinctively rise to defend them.

Further, the act of valuation implied by the word "higher" defies the charge of subjectivity. One might say that the ideal of free personality within a free society suits our disposition and our background, and therefore we like it; but, one might continue, there have been plenty of other societies in other circumstances where freedom of personality was subordinated to solidarity for the sake of power or wealth or pride or even fear, and the people in those societies liked their systems as much as we like ours.

First, there is no solid reason to think so. Second, such societies were tolerated despite, not because of, their lack of freedom. Third, the people were generally unaware of the price they were paying. Fourth, such societies have proved inferior by quite objective standards. In the somewhat sickly relativism, and the salutary self-criticism, that color Western thought, it is easy to lose all magnitudes and distinctions in a murky gray. It is well that we should be humble and modest about our achievements; and the more clearly we apprehend our ideal, the more humble and modest we shall be. It is not well that we should thereby become muddled or equivocal about the ideal itself.

Wisely indeed did the founders advise "a frequent recurrence to fundamental principles." Every idealist goes through periods of lassitude and discouragement in which he is tempted to doubt the validity and worth-whileness of his most vital intentions. Those are occasions to which all further argument is inadequate, when what is needed is a bold and apparently unsupported reaffirmation of the original act of will. The classic example is the gospel story of the temptation, which is of course a study in the psychology of power, prefiguring the crucifixion. At the critical moment Jesus does not stop to argue. To the devil's offer of "all the kingdoms of this world, and the glory of them" he does not reply, "They are not yours to give"—as one would think he might have done. He simply tells the devil to go to hell. "And angels came and ministered unto him" because he had made the highest affirmation of which true humanity is capable; and he had made it, as one has to, alone.

The ideal of free personality in a free society rests on a major assumption that cannot fully be argued here or finally validated by all the millions of pages that have been given to it. It is the basic assumption of most schools of natural law; namely, that there are tendencies innate in human nature which make for social harmony in spontaneity. If this is true, not only is freedom a good; it is a good investment. As to how these tendencies are to be emancipated from other tendencies (there are others) and implemented for the common welfare, opinions have ranged all the way from Jean Jacques Rousseau to Pope Pius IX. Indeed, by the 1860's the debate had reached the scale of historical thesis and antithesis. But, as we are now beginning to understand, there is more in common between pagan and Christian philosophies of freedom, especially on French soil, than there is between either of them and the modern rationalizations of tyranny. For they will find themselves in agreement on at least one practical issue: the only authority that can have a final claim upon the obedience of modern man is that which arises from the perception of humanity at its best and finest. The only command that can compel free men is that which calls them to be all that they are capable of being. What the authority of the state finally enjoins is man's duty to himself. This is the only solution of the problem of authority within democracy.

The central concern of the state is therefore, in the widest sense, justice; not power; not even prosperity. The state is the social structure through which our sense of right becomes articulate and effective.

> It is an association of men, occupying a definite territory, in which a common sense of right issues in general agreement regarding the value of both public and private interests. . . . The ultimate law-making power is nothing but human judgment itself acting upon human interests and deciding with reference to their relative value. The state, therefore, is the community acting in its collective capacity to recognize values.[9]

In this sense the state is recognized by philosophers and theologians as part of the natural order: sanctioned by, grounded in, and bounded by, that order. In so far as it truly expresses that order, it has true authority. In so far as it denies or defies that order, it has no true authority and will therefore find itself driven into a wilderness of inhuman coercion; for the natural order is fact, not fiction. It is there to be recognized,

9. H. Krabbe, *The Modern Idea of the State* (New York: Appleton-Century-Crofts, 1922), Introduction by Sabine and Shepard, pp. lxxv, lxxix.

learned, and lived by. One way or another it teaches us what we call the natural virtues (even Jean Jacques, so far as he saw anything clearly, saw that). It does not care how it teaches, and it is never in a hurry, because its teaching must come through our own experience; but it will not allow any false form of human association to stand too long in the way. What it wants, so to speak—and we may speak here on an almost biological plane—is that the human creature shall achieve by his peculiarly human attributes a success in community at least as good as what certain insects and animals have achieved by their attributes. There are plenty of humans who, like Wells in his last years, despair of the prospect, and not without reason. Possibly the human creature, precisely because he is human, must call for supernatural aid. But, on the natural plane alone, it is evident that the very essence and foundation of tyranny (i.e., failure of community) consists in a misapprehension, or a deliberate defiance, of the truth about human nature.

> It is from natural law, and from natural law alone, that man obtains those rights which we refer to as inalienable and inviolable. Man's only right, in the last analysis, is the right to be a man, to live as a human person. Specific human rights are all based on man's right to live a human life. His right to existence, for example, the right to perfect his moral nature, his right to personal freedom, the right to be treated as a free, intelligent, responsible human being in no way depend upon the state.[10]

There is a caveat here to be entered that will be more familiar to theologians than to law students. It will be noted that the above very sound passage does not contain the word "happiness." The American Declaration does not claim "happiness" as a human right (how carefully those men wrote and thought!) but only "the pursuit of happiness." It certainly is that, as witness the Gospels. But the Benthamite teaching,

10. T. P. Neill, *Weapons for Peace* (Milwaukee: Bruce Pub. Co., 1945), p. 155.

with its "pleasure-pain" psychology, overlaid the natural law tradition with a gloss so thick and shiny that it fooled many of his followers. Bentham himself knew what he was doing and finally rejected the whole idea of natural law; he thought he was being more realistic and was disappointed when the Europeans did not agree with him. Modern American thought has tended to revive the Benthamite fallacy; that is, it has tended to inculcate the idea that happiness itself (variously and voluminously defined in radio speeches) is a natural right and therefore constitutes a claim that man—at least American man—may legitimately press against the American state or, failing even that, God Almighty.

No school of natural law supports such nonsense. What the great tradition indicates may be summarized in two propositions: (*a*) every soul is equal in the sight of God (this may mean something to people who believe in "souls" and in "God" if they understand what they believe; but it may be translated as meaning that we are not to discriminate in our personal relations with people according to their external circumstances) and (*b*) the good old maxim, equality of opportunity—which sounds so much simpler than it is if one admits that individuals cannot be dealt with in isolation.

A generation ago it would have seemed superfluous, almost platitudinous, to dwell on this traditional theme in this highly generalized form of it. The Western world, we thought, universally assented to it, with only minor qualifications here and there. We have since seen the rise, with appalling swiftness, of tremendous political systems that reject it root and branch. And are there yet areas of our own land in which members of our own national community are denied the right to be treated as free, intelligent, responsible human beings? If the American state connives at such denial, it cuts the ground from under its own feet to a degree that its enemies do not fail to measure.

This is one of those issues in which we are compelled to distinguish between state and government. The economist is tempted to cut the matter short by saying that, as far as he is concerned, the state is what the state does; but the escape from philosophy is only verbal. The actual doing is done by what we call the government; but to identify the state with the government is neither safe nor sound. Lord Lindsay of Birker in his recent book, *The Modern Democratic State*, points out that we have to meet the question "why men obey certain persons called the government and obey them under certain conditions and on certain understandings. That you cannot do without considering ideals. For the state, like other organizations, can only be understood in the light of men's purposes, in what they are after in their organization."[11]

There is the further difficulty that the state, however we define it, is generally supposed to survive changes of government, even quite drastic ones. It is a pretty tough old bird. Under normal circumstances there is a very simple factor acting to preserve the state from the vicissitudes of politics: it is impossible for even the most enthusiastic of New Dealers to change all the rules and all the habits all at once. In our everyday notion of the state there is a deeply imbedded sense of continuity. A good deal of this, as Lindsay frankly recognizes, is mere inertia. But inertia is only part of the story. What the state means is a certain continuity of norms and purposes to which most of us, when we think about them, give a general assent, not merely for the sake of peace and order but for the sake of—well, we can hardly beat the phrase "a more perfect Union." To this complex of norms and purposes Lindsay applies the very useful term "operative ideals"; and he maintains that the practical task of political theory is to make them explicit, bring them into clear focus.

11. A. D. Lindsay, *The Modern Democratic State* (New York: Oxford University Press, 1948), p. 38.

We arrive, then, by what is really a dialectical short cut, at the following position: a government (which means certain persons making decisions and giving orders) derives its authority not merely from the particular circumstances of its appointment (which may be quite peculiar, since the phrase "consent of the governed" may now mean anything or nothing) but from the fact that it is the recognized embodiment here and now of the state. Since the state itself is a matter of will and purpose (which again means human beings willing and purposing at a deeper level), the acts of government are subject to a double check. There will be, first, the question of how far, or how efficiently, these acts define the operative ideals that really constitute the state; and there will be, second, the continuous critique of those ideals themselves, in which the government of the day may itself be a challenger. We have a cogent illustration of this in the fact, which Lord Lindsay notices, that, when we set out to discuss such a topic as the economic role of the state, there arises a general expectation that we shall consider not only what the state, via government, is doing and can do but what it ought to do. How are we to know what it ought to do? I shall not attempt to evade that question, for it is the question in which we are all supremely interested.

One more distinction is needed. We have to bear in mind not only the relation between state and government but the relation between state and society. Here again we must ignore a vast and fertile field of political philosophy to take a dialectical short cut.

Society is obviously more than the organized aggregate of human beings living at this moment, though even that seems to be disintegrating. Urban society shows an increasing tendency not only to institutionalize the children but to institutionalize the grandparents. The typical home of earlier generations, like the rural home of today, was much more likely to have a place for the old people than is the modern urban domicile. Further, it may reasonably be held that the concept of society covers not only three living generations but also to some extent those who are no longer present. There is at least the simple fact of their testamentary dispositions. A very able British conservative maintains that it is not open to the state (not merely the government) to falsify or abrogate expectations that it has made legitimate either by express permission or by tacit consent.[12] That clearly covers the relations between the generations; it puts the continuity of the family into the foreground of the picture; it implies a very serious criticism of current British practice.

Society, as many people think of it, can no more exclude the dead than it can ignore the unborn; it is in fact a continuum of human relations that is never wholly contained in its material aspect. What relation does it bear to that continuum of operative ideals which we call the state? Put in this way, the question admits of only one answer. Society is prior to the state, not only historically but axiologically—prior in time and in value. The state exists to maintain and foster those living bonds which keep a true society together; but it does not create them, and, if they die, it cannot of itself revive them. It can destroy them, and there are cases on record when it has done so. Indeed, the abuse or misuse of the coercive power is so constant a risk that there are in pagan, Christian, and anti-Christian philosophies strong tendencies toward limitation and distrust of the state, even where practice tends to exalt it. Possibly there may be common ground here on which something could be built. The possibility is worth exploring.

12. G. G. Butler, *The Tory Tradition* (London, 1914), p. 56.

V

FROM HUMANISM TO PATERNALISM

☼

FEW sentences in economic literature contain more history than that which introduces Book IV of *The Wealth of Nations*. "Political economy, considered as a branch of the science of the statesman or legislator, proposes . . . first to provide a plentiful revenue or subsistence for the people, *or, more properly, to enable them to provide such a revenue or subsistence for themselves*." In that correction lies the difference between two great epochs. In the general introduction to his work Smith had very firmly stated his conviction that it is work rather than legislation upon which the prosperity of any community depends. He is far from indifferent to the conditions of work or to its physical, mental, and moral effects upon the people. But he will not tolerate the illusion that state action as such can do more than clear the way for improved effort and equitable exchange.

Few people today read enough of Adam Smith to appreciate his quality. He is often supposed to be the father of laissez faire, and some of our contemporaries who should know better have thus represented him. But of laissez faire as a system or a dogma, Smith was not even the stepfather. His concern for liberty neither began nor ended with economics; and his defense of the American colonists is by no means the only instance in which, for him, liberty and justice ran together. He would never have urged the former at the expense of the latter, even had he been able to envisage such an alternative. His case for what is now called the economy of high wages does not rest solely on the economy; in this and many another matter he would as lief appeal to "equity" as to interest. His empiricism is that of the true humanist whose eyes no theory can blind to the facts of life; and among such facts those of the moral order, as he conceived it, are never absent from his thought.

In this respect above all he sets the line for the proper economics of freedom. Soon after his death the division began to emerge that continues today among his followers; it coincided pretty closely with the academic recognition of political economy as in effect the theology of money-making. Despite his talk of "science," Smith was by vocation and profession a moral philosopher, as were many of his successors, especially in America; a high proportion were in fact Christian ministers and none the worse for it. But the latent humanism of their attitude was both assailed and undermined by a conception of "science" which excluded the distinctively human criteria. That conception drove an iron wedge between the humanists and the scientists—or, rather, between the "humanism" and the "science," since in many cases the two ideals struggled for mastery of the same mind, as they still do. This struggle is vividly reflected in the history of British social legislation.

Roughly speaking, we may say that in practical matters the victory went to the humanists, while in the theoretic field it went to the scientists. The former included many conservatives and the latter many laissez faire liberals. The empiricism of the former stood at a disadvantage, when it came to argument, against the systemizing of the latter. A bit more system on the one side and a bit less on the other would have made the road easier, but circumstances precluded that approach to a synthesis. Among the critics of the "dismal science" none made more noise than Carlyle and Ruskin; yet even today few students of either could give a succinct account of their social philosophies. They rendered a good bill of particulars; but what in the way of system had they to offer that could compare with the beautiful clarity of J. S. Mill? Were they even, in any definable sense, Christian? Their emotions perhaps were, but was their thinking? Christianity can and does offer a strong and coherent set of social principles when its own postulates are fully recognized and accepted; but, when those postulates are blurred or watered down or rationalized away, it becomes merely one species of subjective idealism among others. This is most embarrassing to many modern Christians whose Christianity is more a matter of sentiment than a matter of fact.

The vindication of humanistic, that is, personal, values against the mechanistic "social science" of the nineteenth century never lacked for talent or persistence. Nearly all the great minds of an exceptionally fruitful epoch were on that side; and in the end their influence prevailed. But their influence was, and still is, weakened by the lack of a common positive philosophy as clear and coherent as that of the mechanists and "positivists." The latter, of course, had the easier task in the matter of system, since they began by discounting all those motives and aspirations that did not fit into the contemporary idea of science. For some of them that involved a considerable strain on the conscience; but such was the spell of system that the trick was turned. In the refracted light of the era it looked plausible; just as did the deliberate destruction of food and cotton in a starving world to the American doctrinaires of the twentieth century. Once you stifle the conscience and eliminate the personal from your calculations, there is no limit to the absurdities to which system can drive you.

The difficulty of social humanism in its contest with social scientism has all along been the lack of an integral philosophy. There is no literature of compassion so great as that which runs from Kingsley and Dickens to Hardy and Masefield; social reform owes more to it than to all the theorists and philosophers. Yet it failed to build Jerusalem in England's green and pleasant land: because the underlying intellectual tradition of Christendom had been allowed to lapse. Ever more clearly in retrospect we see how deeply rooted were, and are, our social values in the Christian heritage; but Victorian Christianity was suffering an intestinal crisis brought on by the starchy diet of the eighteenth century, at the very moment when the Christian tradition was called to meet a far graver challenge than that of Luther or even Calvin—a challenge that struck at its very roots.

In the long struggle to preserve the human values from the tyranny of dynamic materialism, whether through state action or voluntary co-operation, there were good people calling themselves Christians on both sides of every practical issue, including war, slavery, and child labor. Nor were the differences between them merely about tactics and timing; they were differences of principle. Now it is proper that there shall be differences of secular policy between adherents of the same religious faith; the question is how far they may go without rendering the faith nugatory. An instructive case is that of John Bright's opposition to the British Factory Act of 1844. Bright was one of the finest men the Society of Friends has given to public life—which is saying much. The bill of 1844 marked a long step forward in the assertion of a public conscience; it limited the labor of women and thirteen-year-olds in factories to twelve hours a day, with time out for meals measured by "some public clock." Here is what John Bright said about it:

> The people ask for freedom for their industry, for the removal of the shackles on their trade; you deny it to them, and then forbid them to labour, as if working less would give them more food. . . . Give them liberty to work, give them the market of the world for their produce, give them the power to live comfortably, and increas-

ing means and increasing intelligence will speedily render them independent enough and wise enough to bring the duration of labour to that point at which life shall be passed with less of irksome toil of every kind and more of recreation and enjoyment.

It was an odd fact, however, that Bright, unlike his master Adam Smith, opposed the development of trade-unions; but the root of his dilemma was the conviction that the quantity of production was the paramount consideration; and he had before him Mr. Senior's ingenious demonstration that all the profit of industry would be wiped out by cutting an hour off a twelve-hour working day.

The advance of technique and the accumulation of capital have disposed of Bright's apprehensions and Senior's statistics, but we must be careful not to judge either the economic or the ethical issue simply by hindsight. Bright's dilemma was not wholly illusory, for there can always arise situations in which a choice between economic and noneconomic values has to be made and their relative weights and reciprocal bearings decided upon. That is the critical issue on which no merely material calculus can be decisive. As A. C. Pigou has stated, we can take it as a rough rule that what promotes economic welfare will also promote general welfare; but there are so many possible exceptions (when the two concepts are separated) that each case must be considered on its merits. In such consideration people who are muddled about their "fundamental principles" are handicapped in comparison with those who are not, whatever the principles may be.

On the whole, British social legislation "muddled through" in the right direction with a remarkable tenacity, led by the ethical co-operation of people of very varied faiths and backgrounds. The detailed record gives conclusive evidence that the basis of effective state action is moral, not material. The various winds of doctrine were blowing a full hurricane in the midcentury, but the common sense of right, *Rechtsbewusstsein*—

what medieval writers called the *communis estimatio*, the common estimate of what was fair and reasonable—proved extraordinarily persistent; so much so that even scholars could forget that it had specific historical roots: this and not that basic conception of the nature of man and society.

The clearest example is the introduction of British minimum wage law. The laissez faire theorists had built a stiff barrier against that much state interference with "business," though not so stiff as in America. In England the real battle had been won as far back as 1833, when the government had successfully asserted its right to send public inspectors into the private property of manufacturers. But wage legislation was a new and radical issue. In 1908 a small group of people who really knew what was going on inside the sweatshops decided to by-pass all theory in the interests of action. They got newspaper support from certain Quaker families; then they hired an exhibition hall in London and reproduced there the actual conditions under which thousands of women were working. It was a direct and effective appeal to the common sense of right. The public felt that, come professors or politicians, dividends or deficits, that was no way for human beings in England to be taking advantage of other human beings. The resulting legislation (of which more will be said hereafter) worked well because it stood on that broad ethical basis. Consequently, state coercion could be kept to a minimum and was pretty sure of support when it had to be applied. Incidentally, there was very little dislocation of industry or employment.

A great deal of what foreigners regard as mere opportunism or empiricism in British policy looks that way not only because it springs from a moral rather than a theoretical instinct but because the moral instinct is specific rather than general, inarticulate except when occasion forces an issue, never definable in terms of code or creed, and therefore somewhat unpredictable in operation. For the same reasons it can be, and often has been, temporarily (but not permanently) perverted by rogues, demagogues, and doctrinaires. On such occasions hypocrisy becomes the outward and visible sign of an inward and spiritual confusion.

Now confusion as to the fundamental principles of morality—personal, social, and national—was the main practical effect of the first seventy years of nineteenth-century thought. It is significant that the best-known pronouncement even of the Catholic church in that period was a list of eighty propositions in the negative, many of them double negatives. Catholics in both America and Europe have inherited a horror of the very word "liberalism" because of the profound confusion it then seemed to cover. Sir Wilfrid Ward noted, at the turn of the century, "the feeling that all religious men must act to some extent in concert if society is not to be dechristianized, and if the forces which are exhibited in terrible caricature by the Anarchists are to be successfully resisted."[1]

Meanwhile the physical and biological sciences had made magnificent advances, and it was only too natural that "social scientists" should try to emulate their success in application to human beings. Up to about 1890 the effort seemed plausible, or at least laudable; but by that time integral humanism (to use Maritain's term) was pulling itself together again and challenging the prestige of secular scientism. Some of the results in other spheres are well known; it is interesting to glance at the changing conceptions of economics.

Alfred Marshall, probably the greatest economist of his time, was certainly the nearest in spirit to Adam Smith, and in his later years he became increasingly aware of his distance from his "classical" predecessors. Some part of their excessive abstraction he explains by a very apt observation: "It is a

1. *Problems and Persons* (London: Longmans, 1903), pp. 374–75.

British habit to leave much to be supplied by the common sense of the reader."[2] But they had left altogether too much, with the result that their system seemed farther away from life than it really was or was meant to be. As an example, Marshall cites J. S. Mill's statement that "Political Economy considers man as occupied solely in acquiring and consuming wealth"—and immediately points out that Mill made no serious effort to adhere to such an arbitrary definition. The excessive "pursuit of abstractions," said Marshall,[3] "is chiefly due to the influence of one masterful genius, who was not an Englishman, and had very little in common with the English school of thought. The faults and the virtues of Ricardo's mind are traceable to his Semitic origin; no English economist has had a mind similar to his."[4]

What, then, was Marshall's own idea of his subject? Economics, he says on the first page of his great work, "is on the one side a study of wealth; and on the other, and more important side, a part of the study of man." The emphasis is reiterated in a later book,[5] where, after an analysis of production, Marshall halts the argument to restate his major theme: "Here, as in every other economic inquiry, we must bear in mind that the only aim of that production is the development of the people in numbers, in health, in strength, and above all, in character."

Marshall's successor in the chair at Cambridge, A. C. Pigou, opened his work on the *Economics of Welfare* with a precisely similar warning: "Efforts devoted to the production of people

2. *Principles*, Appendix D2, par. 3.

3. *The Present Position of Economics* (1885). See *Memorials*, p. 153.

4. Maybe so, but there is no one to whom Marshall's remark about the use of English applies with more force than to Ricardo. The present writer should perhaps add his own *mea culpa;* and A. N. Whitehead could hardly have declined an invitation. I have treated the whole question more fully in chap. ix of the Hazen report entitled *College Reading and Religion* (New Haven: Yale University Press, 1948).

5. *The Economics of Industry*, p. 128.

who are good instruments may involve a failure to produce people who are good men." That could apply to industrialists and financiers no less than to carpenters and coal-miners. Examples of the change in emphasis are abundant both within and without the ranks of professional economists, and, of course, not only in England.

The same reaction was asserting itself at about the same time in America. The abstractive tendency had dominated American thought more than it ever did English, and the reaction, when it came, was all the stronger. What it amounted to was not only the refusal of leading men in both countries to continue treating of human beings as mere scientific objects, or classes, but the attainment of a certain academic respectability for the humanist point of view. Such was the state of "higher" education that that was the more difficult achievement! And despite the work of R. T. Ely, J. B. Clark, T. N. Carver, S. N. Patten, J. R. Commons, J. A. Ryan, and a whole generation of collaborators and students, it is even yet too soon to be sure that that achievement was permanent.[6]

For—and this is our main concern with the matter—the recognition of humaner interests than those of the "economic man" raised broader problems, with which none of the social sciences was fully equipped to deal. So long as economics could be regarded as a self-actuating system, run by the "inexorable laws of supply and demand," checked only by "friction," automatically oiled by "mobility," boxed in the clause "other things being equal," and consigned to the "long run," economists could write textbooks and businessmen could make

6. The battle of the schools in America deserves far more attention than it usually gets in institutions of learning and is rich in contemporary significance. Three books constitute a good survey: Richard Hofstadter's *Social Darwinism in American Thought* (Philadelphia: University of Pennsylvania Press, 1944); R. T. Ely's autobiography, *Ground under Our Feet* (New York: Macmillan Co., 1938); and J. R. Everett's masterly analysis of Sumner, Clark, Ely, and Patten, *Religion in Economics* (New York: King's Crown Press, 1946).

money without getting in each other's way. The only serious quarrel arose when the businessmen's co-operation in profit-making ran athwart the economists' assumption of competition; and that was argued as a legal problem rather than an economic one. But when not only economists but businessmen started raising questions that the laissez faire mechanism did not raise, let alone answer, they were raising trouble; whether or not they meant to. Such questions belonged in fact to the domains of ethics, moral philosophy, and jurisprudence. These disciplines had been neglected by, or expelled from, American thought since the eighties to an amazing degree, just when the tide in England was running the other way. Even today their claim to a place in American education is frequently met not merely by skepticism but by downright hostility, encouraged by certain American "philosophies" that still have academic prestige. We are determined to be "scientific" even if it kills us—as it probably will.

Many of the earlier teachers in America, like Francis Wayland of Brown and A. L. Chapin of Beloit, had based their competitive economics on the truths of individualistic religion. Their successors generally underestimated both the logic and the value of that connection. But economic society was apparently ceasing to be individualistic, and individualistic religion, in its effort to become social, was becoming secular. All the more easily therefore could midcentury scientism pronounce a *decree nisi*. How many such decrees are regretted when they become absolute! This was such a case.

For just at the time when the revival of humanism was demanding a revitalized moral philosophy, that department of American culture was handicapped by desuetude and confusion. It is significant, for instance, that Ely—who was never in danger of becoming a Catholic—got Monsignor Ryan to summarize the papal encyclicals for an appendix to his autobiography. Ely and his friends were earnestly, indeed passionately, seeking an integrative principle on the proper level; and it was not their fault that they did not wholly succeed. Perhaps it was unlucky that James, Royce, and Santayana wrote such excellent English; it concealed what it could not reveal.

The task of both the economists and the jurists of this period was not merely academic. Circumstances were forcing the pace. With the growth of associations of wage-earners catching up at last, despite many a legal hurdle, with that of associations of investors, the individualistic bases of classical economics, orthodox jurisprudence, and protestant religion were all challenged by the same movement at the same time. The aims and activities of trade-unions could no longer be dismissed as so much irrelevant "friction" in the works of an otherwise self-regulating machine; and people were coming to feel that, even if they could be, they should not be. The work of Ely and his colleagues was bearing fruit in a more general awareness of the problem of social justice. The time was ripe for a "recurrence to fundamental principles." But the job of applying eighteenth-century principles to twentieth-century realities was complicated by what had happened in the meantime. It had to reckon not only with theories but with facts—including some very awkward ones. And the legalistic habit of French and American thought was less pliable than the political tradition of England, where the line between the legal and the political is not so sharply drawn or so strictly insisted upon.

The dogma of individualism was deliberately and thoroughly built into the foundations of modern France. It was prompted, of course, by the abuse of their economic power by the old guilds, many of which had become, by the late seventeenth century, monopolistic corporations; and the Gallican church was widely regarded as one of them. Accordingly, the Declaration of 1789 declares in the most explicit terms that the sole source of authority is the state, that no person and no group may exercise any authority that does not proceed in plain terms from the law of the nation.

So far so good. That sounded like the liberation it was genuinely intended to be. But two years later—two years of crowded experience and violent emotion—the doctrine was spearheaded toward economic organization in particular. By the *loi le Chapelier*, citizens of the same trade or calling, whatever their status, may form no association, temporary or permanent, may make no joint decisions, may formulate no rules as to their "pretended common interests," may maintain no officers or records, may not even deliberate on common plans to affect the terms of employment; to do any of these things is made a criminal offense, and to instigate them involves also the loss of citizenship. The very "spirit of association" is outlawed—and all in the name of liberty. The dogma was implemented by the provisions of the Napoleonic penal code, which, like the English law of the period, differentiates between the criminality of employers' and workers' combinations. The state is already intrenching its own monopoly against the people.

After the episode of 1830 there was in France a further stiffening of the individualist dogma, which had now become, by its inherent logic, the monistic theory of the state. No association, whatever its size or purpose, might exist except by license of the government. That provision stood until 1884. Then it was at last lifted in respect of "industrial associations"—either of employees or employers—whose object was "the study and defense of economic, industrial, and agricultural interests."

But by 1884 the damage had been done. The grant of freedom of association in the sphere of economic life was a liberal one and opened up possibilities which were in fact widely utilized; but the long experience of suppression had by that time engendered an underlying antagonism between organized labor and the highly centralized state, which has remained a basic ingredient of French politics to this day. For in the meantime the wage-earners had studied the gospel according to St. Marx.

Furthermore, there remained the question of organized religion. This matter was by no means as intrinsic an obstacle to unity as it appeared in the second half of the nineteenth century. New life was striving to break through both Gallican, Jansenist, and Ultramontane traditions, giving rise to internal controversies that were full of difficulty and promise. But the monistic claims of a highly centralized state confronting a highly centralized church exaggerated the problem and frustrated a synthesis. The very keenness of the French mind precipitated a long crisis in which both church and state were losers. The great encyclical of Leo XIII, *Rerum novarum* (1891—a notable centenary), must be read as it was meant to be read, against the background of dogmatic individualism on which nineteenth-century France was so explicitly based. Of course, Leo was concerned about the status of religious associations; but as the custodian of a social tradition that was somewhat older than the French Revolution (or even the Catholic church) his interest was not merely parochial. And he knew the difficulties that the state itself was confronting in the sudden upsurge of economic organizations. "Associations of every kind," he said, "and especially those of working men, are now far more common than heretofore. There is a good deal of evidence which goes to prove that many of these societies are in the hands of secret leaders, and are managed on principles ill-according with Christianity and the public welfare; and that they do their utmost to get within their grasp the whole field of labor, and force working men either to join them or starve." That was 1891, not 1948! But, despite the risks, Leo XIII was willing to contest the absolutist claims of the monistic state in the name of freedom of association for all. Private societies, he says, "cannot be absolutely, and as such, prohibited by the State. For to enter into a society of this kind is the natural right of man"—notice the direct challenge to the individualistic dogma of the Revolution—"and the State is bound to protect natural rights, not to destroy them; and if it forbids its citizens to form associations, it contradicts the very principle of its own existence; for both they and it exist in virtue of the like principle, namely, the natural tendency of man to dwell in society."

Again, so far so good. Liberals, moderate socialists, trade-unionists, and Catholics could all agree on the principle. To that extent the dogmatic basis of nineteenth-century France was in course of being brought up to date. The pluralists saw the light and rendered valuable service, not only in France but in Germany and England—Gierke and Troeltsch, Maitland, Figgis, and the guild socialists. We all felt that a constructive and logical alternative to the monistic state was in the making, a new vision of a functional democracy, in which personal liberty could be fulfilled in a harmony of voluntary group action that would enrich the cultural as well as the economic life of an associative society. It was a fine dream while it lasted.

But what followed? A generation not of peace but of war on both fronts. Within less than twenty years after Leo's famous pronouncement, M. Briand, himself a former advocate of the general strike, was using the military strength of the French state to crush the strike of the railwaymen. The contest was renewed in 1920, with the state successful by the same methods—22,000 railwaymen dismissed, 700 prosecuted or imprisoned. The contest continues. It is rather magnified than mitigated by the fact that the state has proclaimed itself the owner of certain basic industries and services, for the effect of such action, in France and in other countries, is simply to transform what might have been an ordinary industrial dispute into a dispute between the workers and the state itself, with political and perhaps revolutionary overtones. It then becomes easy to represent labor unrest as treason or revolution; but it also becomes easy to persuade discontented workers, pressing demands which their employer is in no position to meet, that the state itself is their enemy. Then arises a desperate impasse. The state may raid the assets of other economic groups to pay the price of survival; it may rely, for the time being, on straight cash subsidies from other states interested, for their own reasons, in maintaining the status quo. Neither expedient can be more than temporary. At the end of that road lies dictatorship of some sort, based on the plea of holding the national community together. The most effective basis of that plea—perhaps the only effective basis—is the allegation of a national enemy. Both the plea and the allegation will be disputed, in deed as well as word; and by such tragic means the monistic theory of the state—the inevitable outcome of individualistic dogma—meets its historical nemesis.

The English have so far escaped the crisis by virtue of their well-known intellectual limitations. They are never at ease when abstract principles are taken too seriously as a basis for politics. Neither individualism nor laissez faire influenced the course of English history as much as foreigners suppose, who merely read the literature. The atomistic society that French doctrinaires had decreed for their country prevailed in England for just ten years, and even then more by accident than design. The distrust of workmen's combinations reached its climax in the repressive legislation of 1799, whipped up as usual by the fear of national insecurity. But there remained on the statute-books the bulk of the Elizabethan code and a host of supplementary laws, by which the state took a positive responsibility for the level of real wages. It was to these laws that the victims of the industrial revolution kept appealing: the employees were the conservatives; the employers, armed with the new technology, the radicals. The situation came to a head in the great debate of 1813–14, and the employers won, using the plea of freedom.

The position then was that, while the workers were forbidden, under pain of criminal indictment, to combine for self-protection, the state had washed its hands of all concern for them. That situation was too inequitable to last, whatever the doctrinaires might say. It is noteworthy that some of the men who worked hardest to repeal the anticombination laws were themselves quite skeptical of the actual value of trade-unions. Nonetheless, the right to freedom of association was triumphantly asserted in 1824. Its historic novelty was compensated by a series of laws about the nature and consequences of acts done in concert; but, despite practical blunders, revolutionary fiascos, legislative hurdles, and legal misgivings, British labor proceeded to teach the world a lesson in collective bargaining.

Yet even in Britain the problem presented by the right of free association was not finally solved. As in other countries, so soon as the state found itself hard pressed by the price of international anarchy, it passed the pressure on to subordinate groups, by fair means and foul. The first crisis in Britain came promptly in 1919, when Lloyd George beat the railwaymen by tactics very similar to those he had used in the recent election. Then came the official betrayal of the miners, leading inevitably to the general strike of 1926. That strike would never have generated its force if the politicians had not so cynically shown themselves to be liars, but it gave the reactionaries their long-awaited opportunity. The government, in its official newspaper, now dramatically described the striking workmen as "the enemy"—the tone was that of a master-rhetorician—and by the confiscation of newsprint and the control of the radio did its best to engender the war psychology that always gives the rhetorician his finest occasions. Criticism, including that of the Archbishop of Canterbury, was ruthlessly suppressed, and pleas for peace dismissed as appeasement. Convoys of tanks, armored cars, and machine guns were dispatched into the industrial areas, backed by the use of the navy at the ports; and, if the situation failed to develop into civil war, it was not the fault of the Chancellor of the Exchequer, who personally and bluntly announced the doctrine of unconditional surrender. Perhaps it is fortunate for the remnant of the British middle class that the present Socialist government possesses no leader with the amphibious genius of Mr. Churchill.

Of course, it can't happen here? But it has happened. We have become almost accustomed to government seizure of plants, industries, and services threatened by labor troubles; and it is not merely a wartime development. Fortunately for all concerned, such measures as the government seizure of the mines in 1943 and the three military controls of the railroad system in 1944, 1946, and 1948 have been accomplished—so far—with no weapons more dangerous than a fountain pen. We hope that pacific disposition will continue; but as we find the conduct of our economic life, both domestic and foreign, increasingly at the mercy of a particular type of interest group, we may begin to wonder. When cargoes for Europe under the Recovery Plan of the American government have to depend on the army to move them; when trade-unions assert their power, rightly or wrongly, to decide what goods, if any, shall go to what destinations on what terms—then the right of free association promises at least as much trouble to the state in the twentieth century as did the right of personal freedom in the eighteenth; so much, in fact, that we have seen it forcibly abolished in a large number of modern states, including Russia.

It is evident that the economic role of the state in a society controlled by associations rather than by individual persons presents problems in both practice and theory that are not yet solved. Anthropologists as well as philosophers are agreed that the unsocial individuals on whom Hobbes based his myth of the state never existed outside his own imagination. But unsocial as well as social groups—that is, groups based solely on self-interest as well as groups inspired by a conception of the common good—are a fact too obvious to refute. It may almost be said that no group organization can embody a full range of personal interests and sympathies; it is certain that no purely economic organization can do so. A good deal of our present difficulty arises from a modern myth much more effective than that of Hobbes; namely, the American myth that an association of mere investors is a person within the meaning of the Constitution and may plead the immunities of the Fifth and Fourteenth amendments against any particular control demanded by its particular nature. That piece of legal mythology is almost enough to make one accept the Marxist interpretation of history. But it has been matched by another; namely, the myth that an association of wage-earners, powerful enough to hold the entire community as hostage until its demands are met to its own satisfaction, has no legal existence or liability whatever.

Those who, like Leo XIII, defend the right to freedom of association, now find themselves forced by facts into a very difficult dilemma. They are compelled to inquire more closely under what circumstances, or conditions, unlimited freedom of association promotes the common good—or the common ill. The liquidation of individualist dogma was a necessary step forward toward a more humane society and a useful check on the trend toward the monistic state. But by itself it solved no fundamental problems. Human purposes are not necessarily purified or ennobled by being pursued in association; they merely gain a higher potential, for better or worse. The reader may ask himself which way, on the whole, it has gone in our

ime and whether there is any general rule or principle of dis-
:rimination between types of associated action.

Just as the transition from an individualistic to an associa-
:ive society eliminated old inequities at the price of new prob-
ems, so did the transition from the negative to the positive
idea of the state. In no sphere of political discussion is there
more confusion of thought than in this, and it is necessary to
emphasize certain broad historical distinctions.

First, there is the extreme position of the early nineteenth century that the state as such has no responsibility for, and therefore no concern with, the conditions of life and labor. It is to be noted that this thesis, while not without significance, had no extreme urgency in a society that was mainly agrarian and handicraft, simply because agriculture and the crafts are by their very nature systems of personal relations. It was the dominance of trading capital and the ensuing spread of factory employment that made the negative doctrine so radical, so inhuman, in effect.

Second comes the stage we glanced at earlier in this chapter: the stage in which private conscience, eliminated from an impersonal economic system, reasserts itself through the medium of public law. Here of course its demands are minimal and negative: the fencing of machinery, some sanitation, getting children and young women out of the mines, a limit on hours of work, etc. This is "protective legislation" in the sense that it supplies some measure of the protection that a personal relationship might in other circumstances be expected to give. But just for that reason it is not in principle class legislation; it is merely the implementation of what everybody may be supposed to desire. Critics of the method, like Bright and Cobden, did not dispute the end in view; those who, like Spencer, disputed the end in view postulated a different sort of humanity.

Third, however, comes the stage in which specific groups or classes as determined by economic status (usually measured in monetary terms) are made the objects of positive legislation for which other groups, or all groups, have to pay. Now, in contrast to the occasional procedure called for in the second stage, the coercive power of the state steps into the foreground and becomes ubiquitous. The object now may be to purchase popular support for a particular political regime; but it may also include a genuine attempt to equalize economic risks or a more questionable attempt to equalize, by coercion, economic advantages. The capital levy of 1948–49 in Britain was a clear case of the latter.

From this the fourth stage naturally follows. If the state may use its power for the benefit of particular groups or classes, surely, in a democratic system, it will be still more justified in using its power for the benefit of all? This is the dawn of womb-to-tomb security, hailed as the fulfilment of humane politics and the culmination of liberal aspirations. It sheds a new light on both history and political philosophy, as in the following quotation from an eminent idealist:

> In the nineteenth century the individual had comparatively few liberties. There was no recognition that the government owed an individual certain things as a right. There were charities, but at that time the government was not conceived as doing away with charity. Now it is accepted that the government has an obligation to guard the rights of an individual so carefully that he never reaches a point which needs charity.[7]

The philosophy of "rights" herein exhibited is perhaps the basic New Deal contribution to political thought. It had already been announced by President Roosevelt in a speech of October 28, 1944,[8] which enumerated the most extensive collection of "rights" that any responsible statesman has ever

7. Mrs. Eleanor Roosevelt in *Ladies' Home Journal*, July, 1948. Reprinted from *The Ladies' Home Journal*. Copyright, 1948. The Curtis Publishing Company.

8. Quoted in my *The Liberal Tradition*, pp. 41–42.

advanced. There was hardly a limit to what the government "owed" the individual; enthusiastic listeners saw no connection with what the individual owed the government.

But there is a fifth stage. So extensive a program of good works and benefactions calls for a degree of state coercion greater than mercantilism ever achieved or aspired to. By plausible and popular advances, this neoliberalism saddles itself with a state far heavier-handed than that against which the founders of modern liberalism revolted. But the descent is facilitated by good intentions, and disguised by abstraction; for there is one type of coercion even more ubiquitous than taxation, and that is inflation. Against both types the citizen is practically powerless; and when the former falls short, resort to the latter is inevitable—and easy.

That is not all. When a government discovers that the process of spending other people's incomes has limits that eventually react on their earnings, it begins to reach after the sources of those incomes. When confiscation and capital levies, disguised as taxation, can yield no more, freedom of investment disappears. It goes quietly, because enterprise and venture capital have already been choked off. It is easy now for government to move in on the entire economic system, for the voluntary system has no more fight left in it—which proves the necessity for government operation. No revolutionary action is called for, nothing dramatic or sudden or especially noticeable. In Western countries the voluntary system dies quietly in its attic years before the people begin to ask what has happened to it. After all, they were promised security, at home and abroad; and they forget even that under the spell of fresh excitements.

Once again we must ask whether a "recurrence to fundamental principles" can reveal any rule or symptom by which the critical point in this decline can be made evident—to the few who care.

VI

THE DEBIT ACCOUNT

✲

DURING the year 1948 the American government, through its two million federal employees, was engaged in a multitude of economic operations so vast and varied that it is doubtful whether anybody, in or out of Washington, could frame an over-all picture. These operations were based on a collection of laws, executive orders, and administrative decisions accumulated through fifteen years of depression, war, and inflation to a point at which the right hand of government scarcely knew what the left hand was doing—a condition that promoted neither harmony nor efficiency within the corps of public servants. Amazing degrees of economic authority had come to rest on virtually autonomous bureaus or individuals; and in the absence of effective budgetary or cabinet control it was difficult for anyone—businessman, banker, farmer, labor leader, housewife—to make more than the roughest of guesses as to the economic future. The inherent tendency of popular government to cater to the demands, or emotions, of the more numerous blocs of voters seriatim had the total effect of increasing the amount of uncertainty over and above what nature (including human nature) always provides.

Neither the election campaign of 1948 nor its unexpected outcome did much to make the economic future more predictable. The various interest groups stood round the political banquet board like more or less amicable dogs, half-expectant and half-apprehensive of more favors or more restrictions, more benefits or more exactions. This situation was reflected in the behavior of the stock market, in the attitude of private investors toward both domestic and foreign offerings, in the financial policies of corporations, in the demands of organized labor, and in the apprehensions of the long-suffering "white-collar class"—the sort of people whose quiet desperation had provided the nineteenth century with a couple of Napoleons, and the twentieth with a Hitler. For these people, however, with their growing insecurity, the twentieth century had a new answer: the promise of a state-provided security that no government, from ancient Rome to modern England, had yet been able to furnish on an actuarial basis. That fact, however, would not daunt any government equipped with adequate control of monetary policy, since fresh "purchasing power" could always be "created." Thus a precarious political stability might be attained at the risk of a self-perpetuating financial instability, and the unorganized mass of voters be given its share in the benefactions of the modern democratic state.

Under these circumstances criticism could hardly be popular or politically profitable; for the real critic must necessarily appear a mean and captious fellow, attacking governments whose intentions were all (or nearly all) generous, and whose actions, taken one at a time, were indorsed by powerful groups of deserving beneficiaries. Moreover, there was no over-all policy to criticize, merely an endless series of occasions and emergencies that still permitted everyone to unite, at suitable times and places, in a football cheer for free enterprise. "We are going to experiment," said Mr. Roosevelt in 1933—and "We" did. But there were almost as many hypotheses as there were experiments. "The New Deal," wrote some able observers as early as 1934, "is not an integrated pattern. Rather it is a series of measures undertaken in large part with political motivation, many of which are contradictory in character and purpose. The New Deal is not undertaken under the guidance of a blueprinted, pre-planned layout, but is a response to the group pressures which arose from time to time as the depression generated political and economic crises."[1]

The one assumption underlying all the experiments was a naïve and boundless faith in the power and duty of government to remedy any and every type of economic maladjustment. But neither the circumstances nor the national temper encouraged critical examination of this faith, and those who attempted it went almost unheard; nor was their own philosophy altogether adequate to the task. In the result, sound and unsound policies were inextricably jumbled together, and the greatest obstacle to success was the inconsistency. Thus Mr. Roosevelt's opening declarations for sound money and a balanced budget soon dissolved in a manipulated money and a series of swelling deficits. His expressed intention to raise the domestic price level was followed by a rather pathetic inquiry as to why prices were so high. Two years' active encouragement of business monopoly by the NRA ended in a fresh crusade to enforce competition and an equally active encouragement of labor monopoly. While business price-pegging was once again taboo, government price-pegging by the Department of Agriculture and the Bureau of Mines went to amazing extremes of intricacy and arbitrariness. While "economic royalists" and "so-called international bankers" were denounced, the loan and investment operations of government corporations were steadily, and perhaps wisely, withdrawn from public scrutiny. While dumping of goods in foreign trade was penalized by American law, American farm exports were heavily subsidized. While Secretary Hull continued to work for freer international trade, economic boycott was first privately, then publicly, applied as an instrument of American foreign policy.

One could multiply such contradictions without even both-

1. W. E. Atkins, A. A. Friedrich, and V. Wyckoff, *Economic Problems of the New Deal* (New York: Appleton-Century-Crofts, 1934).

ering, as others have done, to compare the actual statements made by Mr. Roosevelt on the various changes of course. His gay, pragmatic temper and buoyant self-confidence enabled him to embrace a new hope and ignore a past failure in typically American fashion. If there was inconsistency, it was not his alone. Every new tack had its group of sincere and enthusiastic advocates. The so-called liberal and labor press could always find some "little band of wilful men" to blame when experiments miscarried and things went wrong. The many split decisions and some outstanding reversals by the Supreme Court indicated a philosophic uncertainty in the highest quarters. And the abundant personal reversals and shifts of policy among the arbiters of public opinion—editors, columnists, commentators, preachers, professors, propagandists—testified to an instability more general, and more profound, than could be attributed to the personal qualities of any one man, even of a genius in leadership. The crisis of conviction in America was no mere political accident but a historic situation.

That situation persists. There is good reason to suspect that the American people would have welcomed a more piercing debate on fundamental principles, both domestic and foreign, than they were offered in the electoral campaign of 1948. There is no doubt at all that they would have profited by it. But the hard-earned victory of President Truman rested not only on his superiority in the art of campaigning but on the support of the principal organized beneficiaries of the New Deal: on the appeal to benefits already received and the promise of more to come. Every direct democracy reaches this phase sooner or later—usually later, for it is the penultimate phase, the phase from which it is almost impossible to turn back. Once the view of the state as the dispenser of benefits becomes the basis of popular government, criticism becomes politically dangerous and debate on fundamental principles is short-circuited. For the benefits are obviously and immediately desirable, whatever their secondary results may be; and, since the recipients are most numerous, criticism can be—and usually is—represented as mere defense of minority interests. Does not the American Constitution require the state to "promote the general welfare"? What is the state for, if not that?

Obviously, therefore, when or if the provision of more benefits for more people encounters financial or economic difficulties, an increase in state power must be forthcoming; and private interests can hardly be allowed to stand in the way. On what conceivable ground could they stand? It is true that the American private enterprise system can hardly be accused of a failure in productivity. It is true that some three-fourths of the American people, including farmers and organized wage-earners, are absolutely and substantially better off than they were ten years ago, despite the costs of war. The voluntary system cannot be, and generally speaking is not, accused of failure; there is no serious demand for "socialization." None-theless, the providential theory of the state—the view that the state can and should provide even more benefits for the mass of the people than the voluntary system has provided—requires that grounds of attack on the voluntary system be discovered or developed. The many real shortcomings of that system are therefore magnified, and its achievements minimized; and a hodgepodge of hostile theories comes into being to justify the political appeal of a coercive egalitarianism.

Old "underconsumption" theories, dating from long before Marx, are refurbished to suit the occasion. We are told that savings now tend to outrun investment opportunities, though we are not encouraged to dwell on the political and international causes of this phenomenon. Harvard economists assure us that a "mature economy" tends to stagnate, although the Back Bay index of maturity may differ somewhat from that of Chicago and points west. Sophomores of all ages indulge in idealistic orgies about the "underprivileged," tacitly assuming that economic status in this workaday American world is in fact a matter of privilege, an assumption to which any honest study of American history gives the lie. But the tender-minded always have their lines of retreat. Pressed on the facts of life, they impugn the motives. The notion is disseminated that there is something wicked about the practice of taking economic risks and responsibilities in the hope of a net profit and the expectation of a free disposal of that profit. Despite both Calvinistic and Catholic indorsements of such motivation, a vague hostility to the "profit system" is engendered. The admitted shortcomings of its operation are used as a blind to the far deadlier shortcomings of alternative systems. In this atmosphere both intellectual integrity and practical consistency dissolve. Expediency replaces principle, and well-intentioned confusion invites disaster. Masses of people neither believe nor wholly disbelieve in the voluntary system—nor, for that matter, in any other system; and in such a mood stability of purpose is unlikely.

Look at the facts. While there was considerable talk, in late 1948, of new government controls to keep prices down, a tremendous amount of government action and public money was directed to keeping them up. During 1948 the American government intervened, by way of parity loans, guaranties, subsidies, price-support purchases, and other devices, in the markets for wheat, corn, oats, rye, rice, tobacco, cotton, peanuts, potatoes, dried beans and peas, soybean, flaxseed, sweet potatoes, pigs, veal, beef, cattle, sheep, chickens, eggs, turkeys, milk, prunes, raisins, honey, grapefruit juice, sugar, wool—and perhaps other items that the present writer probably, and the general public certainly, has failed to keep track of. It is doubtful whether anyone has a complete list, on account of the jumble of laws, orders, and agencies, most of which act under very loose blanket authority. Current guesses at the cost of all this—which again is nobody's business in particular—run near two billion dollars for the 1948–49 crop year. The government was also heavily involved in commercial shipbuilding, aviation, stock-piling, maintenance of industrial plants and processes deemed essential to war, and the support of innumerable domestic and foreign concerns of all sizes and varieties by loan of (theoretically) public funds. It was engaged, on its own account, in a vast and unreported business of foreign investment and foreign trade, as well as in a meticulous regulation of such activities undertaken on private account. Having (rightly or wrongly) forbidden real estate owners income enough for the bare upkeep of their properties, the government was committed to a housing construction program of its own, and promising to go much farther, as also in subsidizing education, raising minimum wages, and vastly extending the benefits of social security. International security was calling as usual for a new armaments race, and the government "take" from the current supply of goods and manpower was once again rapidly increasing. Many of the economic decisions demanded by all these good works, including decisions vitally affecting the value of money, were liable to change without notice; yet nobody really wished any harm to private enterprise, least of all a President who knew by experience how hard it is to make a living.

Under such conditions, however, ordinary economic forecasting, on which private enterprise depends, was almost as risky as political forecasting, from which indeed it was now hardly separable. Venture capital, which more than any other factor had created the modern economic standard, was daunted by a new order of uncertainties. For the time being corporation profits, along with labor and farm incomes, were riding the crest of the wave. Whether or when the wave would break, what would happen if it did, was anybody's guess. The public was outgrowing its propensity to believe that somewhere or other, in the enclaves of Wall Street or Washington, were men who "really knew" or could determine what was going to happen. The masquerade of collective control, national and international, barely concealed the fact that human affairs were more completely out of control than they had been for centuries. And millions of middle-aged people were learning the bitter lesson that no efforts of their own, no amount of individual foresight, hard work, thrift, and sacrifice, could assure them even a moiety of the security, the freedom from anxiety, the opportunity for their children or grandchildren, that they had planned for their declining years. Maybe the state or some other institution would take care of them and salvage some of their hopes; it would not be the same. This depersonalization of the life-history, this casual cancellation of individual and family perspectives, is a factor that now affects, and will increasingly affect, every phase of Western culture. When the individual realizes that, no matter what he does, he is virtually powerless to control, by his own efforts, his economic future, then his attitude toward society, and toward the state, profoundly changes, whether for better or worse it is for Americans especially to consider.

The reader will (or should) at once ask what is meant in this context by the expression "better or worse." There is a value judgment implied. The criterion is the ideal broadly expressed above as free personality in a free society: what leads toward that (so runs my thesis) is better, what leads away from it is worse. This means, at a minimum, free choice of training, occupation, and investment (whether of time, talent, or money) both for those who want to be employees and for that much smaller number who want to be, and are able to be, entrepreneurs; and it means in all spheres that the individual, granted freedom of association, is willing to accept the *major* part of the responsibility for his and his family's economic fate. It is argued that the kind of society in which he can and will do so is better, in the fullest sense, than any other kind. Further implications of this ideal will be examined later. Our immediate concern is with the ways in which people react to their present sense of insecurity, instability, and impotence.

The first way is to fight for the restoration, under modern conditions, of the free society. This requires courage based on the renewed act of affirmation. Faith in the free society has been undermined not only by the statists and rationalists but by those academic and labor intellectuals who preach or tolerate the class theory of society, for, in this view, economic freedom becomes merely a battle royal. I am not referring to the Communists, whose importance—apart from the free advertising American policy has given them—is minor; but to that much larger group whose theories and terminology (e.g., the wide acceptance of the term "proletariat") assume the truth of a view which I hold to be factually false and morally pernicious. The campaign for the free society has to be waged in an atmosphere heavily charged with poison gas.

The second mode of response to the sense of insecurity is simply resignation, fatalism, or despair. It is probable that this type of reaction hastened the collapse of the Roman imperial system. It constituted a serious problem for early Christianity up to the latter part of the sixth century. There are significant traces of it in contemporary thought, especially in Europe.

The most general mode of response to insecurity is to transfer to the state the demands that a man formerly made upon himself (this also is conspicuous in the decline of Rome). Since the state is abstract, powerful, and far away, the demands lose nothing in the process of transfer. This stage is marked by emphasis on and extension of "rights" conceived not as claims *against* the state by the human being, in eighteenth-century style, but as claims *on* the state by the dependent citizen—who, despite his supposed impotence and dependence, can and will raise a lot of trouble if the claims are rejected, as witness the history of the Front Populaire.

By accepting and complying with—still more, by encouraging—this popular philosophy, almost any type of government may gain and maintain itself in power. It was the mainstay of the Nazi movement in Germany ever since 1925. The official program of that year, scorning economic logic or consistency (the leaders knew how little such things matter), was a hodgepodge of promises designed to fulfil the aspirations of ordinary people via state action when they had lost the power, or the hope, of fulfilling them for themselves; the promises made to small business are especially noteworthy. The Third Reich succeeded to an amazing degree in fulfilling these promises for a time and at a price. If the majority of people, especially the younger people, were willing to pay the price—or to sign a note for it, which is what they actually did—those in more fortunate circumstances should take warning rather than take umbrage.

The situation of post–World War II Britain is not essentially different from that of post–World War I Germany, but it is in certain respects more desperate. For Germany in the late 1920's there was a genuine chance of economic revival and expansion, on which American bankers and investors staked billions of dollars, not so recklessly as is now commonly thought. For Britain in the late 1940's there is no such chance. Whether the decision of the British government in April, 1939, to give a blank check to the Poles and the Rumanians (of all people) was based on idealistic or materialistic motives, the check spelled bankruptcy, as some of us knew and said at the time. On either count, victory has spelled defeat. For the underlying economic trends were against Britain in the second war as they were not against Germany in the first. American policy should have known this and reckoned with it. In both wars American policy, leading up to American intervention, was decisive from the start; in both sequels American responsibility is therefore heavy. In the former case, as Hjalmar Schacht repeatedly warned both Germans and Americans, foreign loans and investments could constitute no permanent basis of recovery. The same is true in the second case, and the proof is now developing. Modern war itself defeats every contestant; and when it is superimposed on unfavorable trends, a catastrophic situation is precipitated. That is the present situation of Britain.

In view of the great influence of British example on American opinion, especially in regard to the "planned economy" and the "welfare state," it is important to recognize and distinguish the three main factors of current British policy. First, it must be recognized that in the desperate postwar situation, any British government would have had to resort to exceptional measures of control; just as, in any dangerous emergency, an exceptional degree of collective discipline is called for. Planning for austerity was a matter of necessity, not of choice. Hitler's slogan for the Third Reich—"Export or Die"—was even more appropriate for postwar Britain. Further, the hazards and uncertainties of the open export market in trade, exchange and currency controls, tariffs, embargoes, quotas, and innumerable other impedimenta led in the British case, as they did in the German, to an effort to stabilize that market, or some part of it, by bilateral agreements, clearing agreements, barter transactions, and any other devices that might promise some degree of short-run stability. American foreign economic policy is determined as much by politics as by economics; European nations cannot afford that much leeway. Contrary as this may be to American ideals and interests, it is the logic of circumstances which no British government could have afforded to defy. Inherently, it tends toward the

strong state acting in the national interest. If the government happens to be a socialist government, it tends toward a national socialism. What the ultimate result may be, or the ultimate solution, depends on much deeper and slower-acting forces lying outside national control; the immediate fact is that no government can offer pie in the sky as a substitute for bread on the table. Most of the coercive elements of British policy during the last four years have been dictated, at least in broad outline, by facts rather than theories.

Second, however, there is the theoretical program, almost entirely a product of the intellectuals and comprising two distinct ideals—the welfare state and the socialist state. There might be some question as to the relationship between them.

In the British elections of July, 1945, slightly less than half the electorate supported the socialist parties, including Independent Labour, Common Wealth, and the Communists. Conservatives and Liberals together got slightly more votes than Labour—about 12.2 million to 12.0. On the issue of the welfare state, however, the Liberal vote of 2.24 million should rather be reckoned with Labour; on the nationalization issue, the other way. The result was far from being a landslide; but the familiar vagaries of a two-party system operating with more than two parties gave the socialists 60 per cent of the seats, the first outright majority they had had.

American opinion had greatly overestimated the political weight of Mr. Churchill, whose talents and interests have never lain primarily in domestic affairs. But his party—if it can be called his, since he was no more an orthodox Conservative than his father—had (and has) very able men of the younger generation and an interesting record of achievement. The nationalization of mining royalties, the grid scheme of electricity, the educational program, the agricultural program, and the social security program based on the *first* Beveridge report convey a very different picture of British conservatism from what the average American has in his mind.

But after ten years (and such years!) many voters wanted a change; and new voters, of whom there were over two million, are inclined to vote for new parties just as they did in Germany. The drabness and the misery of the past decade were now clamoring for compensation. The younger people were suspicious of anything that looked like a defense of "vested interests" (another highly colored term), and the women, who equaled the men in voting strength, demanded a prompt restoration of decency in living conditions and a better chance for their babies. The concrete irrationality of women is perhaps a necessary counterpoise to the abstract rationality of men. Thus the 1945 election presented a typical here-and-now challenge, such as crisis always brings, to long-run trends and long-run principles.

In the latter sphere—the only one in which liberalism might have put up a real fight—the party had sold out to the statists by its official adoption of the *second* Beveridge report in January, 1945. This report makes the state responsible for the level of employment (at satisfactory wages) and argues that in order to fulfil that responsibility the state must have full control. It advocates the nationalization of the Bank of England (since accomplished) and wholeheartedly indorses deficit financing. All investment is subject to a state veto, and the state itself is to undertake most of it. The survival of private enterprise depends on a very slender thread, and private property in the means of production exists only on sufferance.

There was a sharp struggle within the Liberal party over the indorsement of this program. The "bow-and-arrow liberals," as Sir William (now Lord) Beveridge called them, rightly saw in its exaltation of the state an abrogation of basic liberal principles. They regarded it as promising all the handicaps of bureaucratic control without whatever benefits there might be in genuine socialism. But the party president, Lady Violet

Bonham-Carter, was an ardent admirer of Beveridge, and the party leaders thought that the scheme was a vote-getter; failing to see that people who really wanted that sort of change would vote for the only party that had a chance of putting it over, while those who did not want it would be driven off to the camp of the young Conservatives. In the result, Lady Violet, Sir William, Sir Archibald Sinclair (party leader), Sir Percy Harris (chief whip), and many others were repudiated by their own constituencies. Tactically speaking, it served them right. A bold reassertion of liberal principles might have stood a chance; but not this academic hybrid.

The Labour party had also indorsed the second Beveridge report but quite logically pulled the control features into its over-all scheme of state socialism. It is doubtful whether the full socialist program ever enlisted as much support even among trade-unionists as did the benefit promises of the welfare state; the electorate was naturally more interested in what it was going to get than in how it was going to get it. That was the government's business, just as it was for the Blum cabinet in France and the New Deal in America. By the summer of 1949 it was possible to see how the business was faring.

The costs of the social services, over and above contributions, were then taking more than 26 per cent of government expenditures. They were bound to go higher with the increasing average age of the population, and the Minister of Health had already found it necessary to warn the people to go slow on their demands; but it is difficult for anyone, when cost (via taxes) is not directly related to benefits, to resist the impression of getting something for nothing and the temptation to demand more than prudence would sanction. Armaments and war preparations, though heavily cut in recent years, were taking in 1949–50 about another 23 per cent of the national budget. Another 15 per cent was taken by the food subsidies, to which Sir Stafford Cripps, in his budget speech of April 6,

1949, drew special attention. The cost of this item was almost as much as the total amount spent on education, health, and housing. These subsidies were based on the principle of maintaining artificially low prices to the consumer with the government making up the difference of high costs to the producer, importer, or processor. The principle was a sound and necessary war measure; its continuance in peacetime (if we may call it that) was an almost irresistible temptation to a popular government. "Now," said the Chancellor, "that just cannot go on. We must call a halt . . . prices have got out of all relationship with realities." He clamped an over-all ceiling on further subsidy expenditures for the year 1949–50 and added that, "whatever happens to prices, we must not allow them [the subsidies] to rise above that level."

There was an open question whether what was left of the budget would suffice to support current commitments, meet foreign deficits, and supply the minimum capital requirements of the nationalized industries. Those industries had not so far proved an asset to government finances. Taking into consideration the terms of expropriation, it was never quite clear whether they were intended to be. Theoretical planning lacks the specific sharpness of business planning, tending to fall back on general theses backed by the power of coercion, and this makes realistic economic operations or forecasts very difficult. If it were supposed that nationalization meant the elimination of nonfunctional gains, the government was now faced with heavy demands for capital re-equipment of its own industries which it must meet mainly out of taxation. If it were supposed that nationalization meant rationalization, the labor government faced stiff labor resistance to the necessary labor displacement. If it were supposed that, despite these difficulties, a cheaper and more general distribution of goods and services would result, the average citizen would pay for it in the diminution of his free spending income; and he might balk at the price. There were signs, both in England and America in late

1949, that he would. One of the basic problems of democratic government is how to manage the interval between the citizen's demands and his own slow realization (it has to be his) of the necessary costs.

In Britain that interval had been prolonged by the common assumption, especially in regard to cradle-to-grave security, that the government, using its coercive power to redistribute national income, could saddle most of the cost on "the rich." The idea is familiar in British history since the days of John Ball and Wat Tyler. It has a certain validity, moral as well as well as economic; but, alas, there are never enough "rich." Lord Beveridge recently added his authority to the repeated warnings on this point: "The trend is against us . . . our relatively easy prosperity has gone forever. It is most important that that should be realized, so that we should all get rid of the idea that our troubles are due to the wrong distribution of the wealth of the country."

Coercive egalitarianism was however frankly accepted by the socialist government as a principle of policy. The results are now on record, and the government rather prides itself upon them. A steeply graduated income tax has long been the backbone of British fiscal policy. The standard rate is now (1949–50) 45 per cent. On this there was superimposed, in 1948–49, a special tax on investment income which in effect was, and was acknowledged to be, a capital levy. On higher income brackets the total tax ran well over 100 per cent of gross income. A man with wife and two children, getting an investment income of $36,000, was liable for a tax of $37,500. A bachelor with $100,000 of such income had to find $130,000. This of course meant throwing all kinds of property—land, houses, cottages, farms, furniture, books, art collections—onto a buyers' market. That was done. But it also meant, as it was intended to mean, the transfer of innumerable personal and private social responsibilities to the state. That was done too. Now the state has them. The Inland Revenue Commissioners, in their report for the year ended March 31, 1949 officially state that there are now only seventy people left in Britain with incomes after taxes of more than $24,000. Quietly as this result has been accomplished, one would have to look back to the French or Russian revolutions for a comparable precedent. But you cannot kill the same goose twice. Coercive egalitarianism has gone about as far it can go; and total taxation, said Sir Stafford in his budget speech, is still taking more than 40 per cent of the national income. What comes next? This is how the Chancellor stated the dilemma:

> We are thus faced with a choice as to how we should distribute the national product. There are many who suggest that we should allow the individual, the wage earner, the salary earner, and the profit earner, more to spend for himself by reducing the charge upon him by way of taxation. But that can only be done at the expense of the Social Services or of our defense.

The key word in this statement is of course the "we"—"how *we* should distribute the national product." Who are "we" and just what is our mandate? "We" are a government to whom, for the time being, is delegated by a narrow margin of the popular vote the authority of the state. "We" have *pro tanto* permission to legislate, on the above lines, subject to retrospective electoral confirmation. But there are underlying factors—historical, psychological, spiritual—that a wise government will bear in mind, for they are the ultimate determinants of social norms and social structure. They are not immutable; but they do not and cannot change as rapidly as do governments and programs. Too great a disparity between the rates of change produces underlying strain, with curious and sometimes dangerous effects. The understanding of these deeper factors is therefore not less important to practical politics than that of the current problems any government has to face. It was this common understanding between leaders of rival parties that gave British politics its extraordinary stability from Burke to Asquith.

The same consideration is now relevant to the United States, where there exists a much greater confusion. Current British policy, whether sound or not, rests as we have seen on three quite explicit bases: the extension of state controls from wartime into the scarcely less exigent circumstances of "peace"; the promise of vastly increased benefits for the masses at the expense of "the rich" which usually follows a war (one recalls Lloyd George's 1918 election promise of "a land fit for heroes to live in"); and the theory of state socialism. American policy can hardly be reduced to this or any other coherent set of principles. In that respect even the top-level advisers of the much-magnified Executive are not in agreement; the Congress splits zigzag, and party labels and programs are in the pressure cooker. But on one point there seems to be widespread agreement; namely, the use of the coercive power to redistribute national income in favor of certain economic groups according to an *ad hoc* combination of criteria, of which voting strength would appear to be the chief component.

This policy, or practice, was backed by the almost casual rejection by President Truman, in July, 1949, of the aim of a balanced budget: a gesture that would horrify even the British Chancellor of the Exchequer. As the National City Bank of New York remarked, in its *Letter* for August:

> If we accept the philosophy that we cannot afford to balance the budget except at the peak of the business cycle, then plainly the budget will remain unbalanced most of the time. The occasional surpluses will be offset many times over by the succession of deficits, and the debt, instead of being reduced, will mount higher and higher. How long we could keep this up is impossible to say, but history is full of examples of the wreckage of currency systems resulting from such improvident policies.

In other words, even to the United States there may come a day of reckoning; and no government can time its arrival.

VII

DISTRIBUTIVE JUSTICE IN ACTION

☼

IT HAS been suggested, in the foregoing pages, that the recent vacillation of American policies, both foreign and domestic, was symptomatic of uncertainty and confusion at a deeper level, often experienced as a sense of crisis in individual minds. The "fundamental principles" and "self-evident truths" on which this community was founded were, I said, in the nature of actions rather than propositions—deliberate affirmations of a system of values that embodied a choice, not merely an argument. As a distinguished modern scholar puts it, "ultimate goals are established by acts of will."[1] In this sense, fundamental principles are not things inherited and kept under glass; they survive, if they do survive, by a continuous reaffirmation, of which the state is the supreme secular vehicle. Its authority derives from this function and is therefore moral in so far as the principles themselves are moral.

But can we discuss whether they are or not? Is there any basis for such discussion? Yes, I said, there is: The development of free personality in a free society is a criterion accepted and extolled even by the economists. (There may be some who contend that it cannot be done on less than six thousand a year, but I will adduce good New England evidence that it can.) There are, or have been, social systems that do not accept this goal as an absolute. They are inferior systems. Undefined as the goal may seem at present, by contrast with all such sys-

1. F. Kaufman, *Methodology of the Social Sciences* (New York: Oxford University Press, 1944), p. 203. Dr. Kaufman is here summarizing the philosophy of Max Weber, with which on the whole he is in agreement.

tems it can become almost at any moment dangerously clear.

It follows that a cardinal principle of policy is the elimination of coercion from all normal situations of social life and that the increase of coercion is too high a price to pay for no matter what collective ends. This is the point at which the defense of freedom begins to be called reaction by state planners, collectivists, and militarists; the point at which the opposition starts its competitive bidding. And it goes high. It counts on the bankruptcy of the older individualism and on the unsolved problems of associative and nationalistic society. It abjures the totalitarian solutions and in the same breath alleges the necessity of over-all planning authorities, national and international, backed by force, thereby tacitly dismissing the ideal of a voluntary harmony in either sphere.

But how or why should anyone believe in that any longer? It is not enough to ask whether the coercive method has been having much luck lately (national or international). The real difficulty is that the postulates of the voluntary system lie on a much deeper plane than that which is usually recognized. For this neglect American education, as it has developed in the twentieth century, bears a tremendous culpability. It has casually assumed, with one or two notable exceptions, that a thousand years of Western thought before Locke could be ignored. That fact has done more to separate Americans from Europeans than all the diplomatic blundering. Europe and America no longer speak the same language. Words cease to mean the same things. The big ones now mean nothing.

If it be accepted as a fundamental principle that coercion in all its forms should be reduced and held to a minimum, invoked only for exceptional cases or causes, some other basis of order must be relied upon. That basis, I have suggested, is moral rather than economic. We give the state a monopoly of coercion in order to get rid of coercion; and we put justice, equity, and compassion above wealth, power, and prosperity as the supreme ends of policy, not only because our tradition so teaches, but because we can get a larger measure of voluntary assent to those ends if we seriously try. It will not be easy, in view of the excessive sectarianism of American thought and the strength of conflicting interests; yet in both theory and practice this approach is still the more promising one from the standpoint of freedom.

In the days when men thought more seriously and systematically about these issues, two broad categories of justice were developed regarding economic affairs: *distributive* and *commutative* justice. These categories are still useful for the organization of both thought and action. I take their definitions from an eminent modern authority:

> Distributive justice prescribes rights and duties between the state, represented by political authority, and the citizens. . . . Commutative justice considers persons as equals before the law and regulates their relations, their exchanges, and services from the standpoint of equality of the exchanged goods or of the remunerations for services. This is the field of justice concerning prices or exchanges.[2]

The distinction is cardinal to the working of a free society, and a good deal of our current confusion is due to our having got the two categories mixed up. By clarifying our ideas of justice, we may widen the area of agreement as to our practical economic policies or at least set decent limits on our disagreement. For a long while now the American people have been eating cake; if now the time approaches when we must eat bread, we can, if we will, make sure that it is the good bread. As Monsignor Ryan wrote in 1916:

> We are not likely to make great advances on the road of strict justice until we acquire saner conceptions of welfare, and a more effective notion of brotherly love. So long as men put the senses above

2. H. Rommen, *The State in Catholic Thought* (St. Louis: B. Herder Book Co., 1945), pp. 148, 185.

the soul, they will be unable to see clearly what is justice, and unwilling to practice the little that they are able to see.[3]

Let us consider first the practical meaning of distributive justice. At the outset we have to notice a modern imbalance. From the French Revolution to the New Deal most of the talk has been about rights and very little has been about duties. Yet in our practical affairs we do in fact assume a bundle of duties corresponding to the modern bundle of rights, because without such correspondence a free society simply could not carry on. For example, we confer protection of the law and we expect conformity with the law; we provide educational facilities and expect parents and children to make the most of them; we recognize the rights of private ownership and expect them to be used with due regard for the common welfare; we establish minimum standards of wages and working conditions and expect employees to show reasonable industry and regularity; we provide the consumer and the investor with lots of information and expect them to take the trouble to use it; we sanction powerful associations of both capital and labor and expect them both to acknowledge the paramount criterion of public interest—and so on all down the line.

It cannot be too strongly emphasized that this reciprocity of rights and obligations is the very foundation of a free society. What I assert as a "right" is not *in essence* my particular interest that I seek to defend against others but a function of our common human nature that is valid for all of us. If it is not valid for all of us, it is not a right but a privilege—and I may be able to defend it, though not on that ground. If it is valid for all of us, we shall be able to agree upon it, and there will be little need for coercion. To be valid for all of us, it must be of some *common* interest or value; and with that admission we

3. J. A. Ryan, *Distributive Justice*, p. 318. Copyright 1916, 1927, 1942 by The Macmillan Company and used with their permission.

turn the other side of the coin, and, lo and behold, it is an obligation! If I assert a right to get drunk on Saturday nights, it must cover all the neighbors. If I say it does so with the exception of Archibald, my only ground can be that Archibald becomes a general nuisance. But that is merely another way of saying that neither Archibald *nor I* has any right to be a nuisance; we have a prior obligation, which may be enforced upon us, to behave decently. Without that obligation the alleged right is nonexistent. Rights and duties are the obverse and reverse of the same affirmations, not different claims that conflict with each other. If they appear to conflict, there is something wrong with the view of human nature that underlies one or both of them. Simple as this sounds, it has far-reaching consequences in the sphere of group action. But if we admit the reciprocity of rights and obligations, the scope of coercion is held to a minimum. And that, if we rate freedom a good, is supremely desirable.

Accepting, then, the postulate that rights and duties go together, and jointly determine our relations to one another as individuals and as groups, we see the mutual relations of state and citizen as a special aspect of a larger whole. Let us remember that, though we give to the state a monopoly of coercion, we do not thereby endow it with a monopoly of valuations. It is merely one among many agencies through which the goals and purposes of human life are brought toward fulfilment. When it acts in its proper sphere with its proper authority, it does so because we have decided that for the particular purpose in view it is the most suitable agency or a necessary adjunct to the others. And the "we" in this decision is not a bare numerical majority or plurality (which may represent nothing higher than a clique of vested interests) but a moral consensus.

Strictly speaking, therefore, it is illogical to maintain that the state *as such* "owes" us anything, in the customary sense of the phrase. Distributive justice does not primarily refer, as does the economic theory of distribution, to the sharing-out of a given supply of goods and services, because the state has no such supply. Yet that is the conception which tends to develop in the late stages of all highly centralized societies, including our own: the notion that the masses can and ought to receive from the state goods and services beyond what they could otherwise earn for themselves. The popularity of this notion has obvious causes, ranging from genuine altruism through political expediency to undisguised class interest. It is noteworthy that, as organized labor becomes a major political force, it is no longer content—as Gompers might have been—to rely on the economic power of the trade-unions but goes on, while resisting all limits on that, to make demands for state action in the interests of wage-earners as a class. And the point is not whether those demands are justifiable as desiderata; quite possibly they are, since, like the king in wonder-working days of old, we would all like everybody to have everything. The point is that this whole notion of the providential state invokes and rests upon the coercive power, regarded solely from the standpoint of the beneficiaries. That is not the true standpoint of distributive justice. Furthermore, there are practical limits to this sort of procedure; and it is less painful to recognize them in advance than to run into them head on.

The power to tax, for example, is the power to destroy, so runs the adage; it is now proved in a novel sense. Classical doctrine taught that the legitimate expenses of government should be levied according to the principles of equality of sacrifice and ability to pay. Some people are always disposed to argue the matter on a *quid pro quo* basis, contending that, since the well-to-do benefit more by legal protection, a soak-the-rich policy is warranted. A slight change in the assumptions would warrant a soak-the-poor policy. Others apply the argument more specifically on a basis of services rendered, where it has some real standing. The upkeep of roads by a tax on gasoline, viewed as a payment by the users of roads, is defensible in so far as motorists drive for pleasure (possibly some still do). But communities as such, and people in them who own neither cars nor trucks, have an interest in the maintenance of good roads; so even in this case the services-rendered principle cannot be applied exclusively. To all such qualifications of the classical rule J. S. Mill made an effective answer a hundred years ago:

> Government must be regarded as so pre-eminently a concern of all, that to determine who are most interested in it is of no real importance. . . . As, in a case of voluntary subscription for a purpose in which all are interested, all are thought to have done their part fairly when each has contributed according to his means, that is, has made an equal sacrifice for the common object; in like manner this should be the principle of compulsory contributions; and it is superfluous to look for a more ingenious or recondite ground to rest the principle upon.[4]

As the system of taxation advanced to its appalling modern complexity, a supplementary canon gained general acceptance; namely, that, as between various alternative types of levy, those which promoted economic equality should, *ceteris paribus*, be preferred. The grounds of this canon, be it noted, were ethical rather than economic. It did not affect the classical principles. The use of the taxing power *primarily* to alter the distribution of national income was not recognized as legitimate practice by any British government prior to 1945. That degree of coercion had been regarded, even by previous labor governments, as amounting to a difference in kind.

And so it has proved. Once a government, in fulfilment of election promises or honest convictions, uses its coercive power deliberately to alter the distribution of income, taking forcibly from this or that group (arbitrarily defined or classi-

4. *Principles of Political Economy*, Book V, chap. ii, § 2.

fied) in order to enrich another (after deducting costs of the requisite bureaucracy), it finds itself embarked on a course of action that is difficult to chart and dangerous to change. If more economic equality is desirable, state coercion is the least desirable way to set about it, not only on account of the technical difficulties and economic uncertainties, but because the plausibility of the aim gives the demagogue and the ensuing dictator their standard equipment for a time of crisis.

It is especially to be noted that, when the economic interests of large masses of people are thus made directly dependent on the state, every economic question tends to become a political question: a situation that makes for both bad economics and bad politics. Major economic issues have to be argued on political grounds, and major political issues are discussed in terms of who gets what out of them. Short as is popular memory, it should be able to recall that in the depression of 1931 the request for a 10 per cent cut in unemployment relief was enough to overthrow the British (labor) government, in an atmosphere of unprecedented bitterness and recrimination. It should also be able to recall the difficulties M. Blum's Popular Front got into less than two years after its formation—and what happened to the franc and the pound sterling. It is extraordinarily difficult in a democracy to persuade enough people that there is anything to be learned from history or that there are any facts at all in socioeconomic relations that cannot be disposed of by wishful politics and generous intentions, implemented by coercion.

In all such matters a cardinal rule of distributive justice is that enunciated by Pope Pius XI in 1931 and sometimes called the principle of subsidiarity. Non-Catholics in America are urged in some quarters to distrust every thesis advanced by the Vatican on the allegation that its assumptions are "totalitarian" in nature and tendency; yet there is no school of thought —least of all the socialist and communist schools—that has so consistently and so thoroughly opposed the aggrandizement of state functions. The argument of Pius XI, even more boldly developed by his successor, is that the authority of the state is degraded and subverted when, and in so far as, it is made the servant of any particular economic interest. "The state, which should be the supreme arbiter, ruling in kingly fashion far above all party contention; intent only upon justice and the common good,[5] has become instead a slave, bound over to the service of human passion and greed." On this ground the theories and practices of individualism and dictatorial collectivism, economic nationalism and finance imperialism, are all condemned; the proper authority of the state is equally subverted when it becomes the tool of an irresponsible wealthy class or of an irresponsible proletariat. There should be no such conflict and no such dichotomy.

How did we arrive at it? Pius XI, in agreement with many non-Catholic observers, put the blame squarely on the dogma of individualism. His statement is so succinct, and at the same time so suggestive, that it merits the serious consideration of all men of good will. Here is the gist of it:

> On account of the evil of "individualism," as we called it, things have come to such a pass that the highly developed social life which once flourished in a variety of prosperous institutions organically linked with each other, has been all but ruined, leaving virtually only individuals and the state. Social life lost entirely its organic form. The state now was encumbered with all the burdens once borne by associations rendered extinct by it, and was in consequence submerged and overwhelmed by an infinity of affairs and duties.
>
> It is, indeed, true as history clearly proves, that owing to the change in social conditions, much that was formerly done by small bodies can nowadays be accomplished only by large corporations. None the less, just as it is wrong to withdraw from the individual and commit to the community at large what private enterprise and

5. It must be noted that the theories of the Marxists, including Professor Laski, deny even this *ideal* of the state.

industry can accomplish, so too it is an injustice, a grave evil and a disturbance of right order, for a larger and higher organization to arrogate to itself functions which can be performed efficiently by smaller and lower bodies. This is a fundamental principle of social philosophy, unshaken and unchangeable; and it retains its full truth today. Of its very nature the true aim of all social activity should be to help individual members of the social body, but never to destroy or absorb them. The aim of social legislation must therefore be the re-establishment of vocational groups.[6]

From this it follows, in the light of subsequent pronouncements and events, that it is better, as a general rule, for the economic status of the wage-earner, as of all others, to be associated with his productive function rather than with his political status. This is a safer rule for politics and a more realistic one for economics. In the more hopeful days of forty years ago, guild socialists had a maxim that "the maintenance of the worker should be the first charge upon industry." It defied the old assumption that mobility of labor was necessary and desirable, and whether it was a sound maxim is still good matter of debate. American practice in the field of public utility regulation has maintained that the maintenance of the *investor* should be the first charge upon industry, and there is much to be said for that contention in a voluntary economy. To argue it out would demand a bigger book than this one. But, whatever the issue, either alternative is sounder and more practicable than the current idea that the maintenance of the citizen should be the first charge upon government. To accept that means that you give up the functional organization of society as a principle of solidarity and accept in its stead a principle that cannot become other than a tyranny, because coercion is its essence. If we can assume a co-operative relationship between the various necessary kinds of economic association, the amount of state coercion is thereby reduced to a minimum;

6. *Quadragesimo anno* (1931).

while, if we cannot assume that, the economic role of the state is enlarged to a degree that has no inherent limits. The proof of this lies in historical facts, not merely in theories.

The way therefore for industry, including that major section of it which is called organized labor, to safeguard its freedom is to accept its full social responsibilities, internal and external, leaving to the state the implementation of our common moral purposes where other means fail or fall short. Those purposes certainly include the intention that none of our community, young or old, shall lack essential sustenance or care through causes beyond his control. This means that public authority shall insure a limit to privation by guaranteeing (not necessarily providing) a minimum subsistence. The policy of the guaranteed minimum is a sound *political* principle because it expresses an almost universal and spontaneous sense of solidarity; and that makes it a *moral* principle rather than an economic one. As such, of course, it is very far indeed from being a novelty in social life. It was morally binding on all earlier Christian communities. The only novelty consists in the fact that the modern state, as representing the largest area of community so far realized, is now getting the moral responsibility. But since its method has to be general coercion on an impersonal basis, the relation between coercion (via taxation) and the moral objective has to be very carefully analyzed. Let us take an exception to prove the rule.

At this writing (February, 1949) large areas of the West have been snowbound since last December. Many communities are without food, water, fodder, fuel, power, and medical care. In these circumstances individuals, voluntary agencies, railroads, the governments of the afflicted states, and the federal army and air force are all co-operating to bring relief; and we in the East are glad to have an over-all agency that can implement our wish to help. There is no question of cost or coercion; no question as to the race, color, creed, or political

ffiliation of the sufferers. They are members of our community
some readers may be able to recall the epic hour-by-hour
roadcasting of the Ohio-Mississippi flood in January, 1937).
But where are the bounds of "our" community on such occa-
ions? If our neighbor countries need such help, do we start
alking politics? If former enemy peoples are so stricken, do
we delay rescue work for a round of foreign-office consulta-
ions? On this plane of action, the state justifies its existence
as a common agent of a common intention, and on this plane
t actually promotes a type of community that has neither
geographical nor ideological limits. This is the ideal type of
democratic action, shining clear in the fierce light of disaster.

I am not, of course, arguing that the state is, or should be, a charitable organization. There is no particular reason why it should not, but we do not in fact feel that "charity" is the right word for action of this sort. Perhaps the Latin *caritas* would come nearer, or the term "solidarity" might serve if it were not now tainted with a certain local and pugnacious flavor. All that, however, is beside the point. The point is that, when the state acts to implement a strong moral consensus, the coercive power is no longer an issue (though it may have to be quite vigorously used), and we all feel better for being able—yes, even for being compelled—to act in concert, so long as the concrete objective has our spontaneous assent. This is a simplified statement of the Catholic thesis that the state, as part of the natural order, has a divine sanction; but it must be noted that the term "natural" is used in a particular sense.

Now consider another contemporary phenomenon, the exact corollary to Mrs. Roosevelt's thesis quoted on page 84. In January, 1949, the British Ministry of Health issued the following statement:

> Now that hospitals in the National Health Service are no longer dependent on voluntary financial help for their normal needs, the

Minister has told regional hospital boards, boards of governors teaching hospitals, and hospital management committees that regards it as improper for them to appeal for funds.

The order specifically prohibits a list of popular activities tha have been part and parcel of English life (and merriment) fo many decades, some of them indeed for centuries. No commen or criticism is here implied as to the efficiency of the stat monopoly; what must be emphasized is the deadliness of it logic. Here is a case where a government, in power by a narrow margin of the popular vote, presumes to *banish* voluntary ac tion; and it must be asked whether, even if the state monopol could be shown to be ten times as efficient, the price would no even then be too high.

It is a safe guess that no American government would be permitted, at present, to go that far; but there is a strong tendency in certain quarters to transfer to the state the major part, or even the whole, of what should be communal respon- sibilities resting on the principle of mutual aid. This tendency is strengthened by the false conception of "rights" already noticed; by the deceptive attraction of the coercive power, which makes all operations seem cheaper and easier than they would otherwise be; and by the widespread confusion as to fundamental principles. If this tendency prevails, it will have effects on the nature of the state, and on its relations with the community, that will be contrary—to say the least—to Ameri- can tradition. It is therefore important that the grounds of objection be clearly realized. This can best be done by reference to certain specific issues.

Let us take, for example, the question of social security, es- pecially in regard to old age. Now the first question to ask, and the one least often discussed, is: What are we aiming at? How much fundamental agreement is there about that? I should estimate that there is not, in America now, anywhere near universal agreement that it is the duty of the state to

aintain old people in general, or any particular group of
iem selected either by income classification or case-by-case
xamination, at a prescribed standard of middle-class comfort.
ut there is, I should think, pretty near universal agreement
hat it is the duty of the state to *make sure that* elderly workers
vhose earnings have been below a certain level be not left to
pend their remaining years in destitution. So we have invoked
he taxing power to set up a minimum degree of insurance to
vhich employers and employees must equally contribute. The
tate does not undertake maintenance; it merely lends its au-
hority and its administrative equipment to make sure that a
ninimum provision for old age is set aside. There is no impli-
ation of dependence on the state; there is no intention to sup-
plant fuller provision made by the individual, the family, the
irm, or any other kind of association. Therefore, in so far as
we are agreed on the necessity of enforcing a minimum provi-
ion, the present system is sound, workable, and legitimate,
and the use of the coercive power fully warranted.

But there is always the temptation to expand its use beyond the legitimate objective. Some young people would like the state to take *all* responsibility for the old folks completely off their shoulders, and so would some employers. Aspiring politicians may hope to gain votes by promising to do so. In such case the principle itself undergoes a radical change, and so does the nature of the society. Of course the specification of the required minimum may have to be altered to correspond with the cost of living—upward or downward—but in the administration of the policy it is all too easy for the idea of complete state dependence to assert itself; and that, as I have tried to show, is the point we have to watch out for.

Similar considerations apply in other spheres, minimum wage law, for example. Here again is a case of the coercive power invoked to enforce what is, or should be, a general moral consensus; and here again there arises a similar tempt tion. As we saw above, the basis of minimum wage law is secure the moral obligations of common humanity against tl inhuman extremes of purely economic motivation. Such w its origin in the competitive economy, national and inte national, of the turn of the century. The need for law aro from the fact that purely economic motivation can driv people, even against their will, into subhuman courses of co duct. To guard against this contingency, we empower th state to punish by criminal prosecution in addition to civ liability employers who fail to comply with prescribed stand ards, and we sanction the incidental risk of putting them ou of business. These are grave powers which should be mos carefully used.

The criteria developed and tested in forty years of Britisl experience are as follows: (1) Each case for the application o coercive powers to a specific, and very carefully defined, trad or industry must be established by factual evidence open tc public argument. (2) Under the original law of 1909 it mus be proved in each such case that wages were "exceptionally low." But since investigation showed considerable areas in which subminimum wages were not "exceptional," the phrase was later altered to "unduly low." This, it must be noted, is an ethical criterion, empirically defined. (3) To this criterion was added, in 1918, the stipulation that there be no adequate existing machinery in the trades or industries affected for the regulation of wages. This marked an important change of policy. The underlying idea was to lift the subminimal groups to a point at which collective bargaining could take charge of the establishment of *standard* rates. It checked the tendency to use the coercive power for that purpose. (4) The foregoing stipulation is retained and strengthened in the legislation of 1945, but the power of the responsible minister to establish what are now called "Wages Councils" is extended over a wider area than that of "sweated trades." The criterion now becomes the ack of adequate machinery to establish and maintain "a reasonable standard of remuneration." The determination of that standard is as before the duty of joint boards of employers and workers, whose decisions, on confirmation by public authority, constitute "statutory minimum remuneration." There were, in 1948, fifty-one such Wages Councils in Britain and eighteen in Northern Ireland, in addition to other wage-regulating machinery operating in the transportation industries, mining, agriculture, cotton textiles, and a few more.

Certain aspects of this development need underlining for American consideration. The determination of specific standards, and of the need or absence of need for their compulsory enforcement, still rests primarily on those engaged in the trade or industry. The Minister of Labour can order an inquiry into a particular field on his own initiative, but he does not usually do so; he waits for an application to be brought up by or on behalf of those affected; and in either case government does not assume the responsibility for fixing the actual terms of remuneration. By leaving that for the people concerned to agree upon, the greater part of the enforcement problem is solved in advance. They know what is reasonable, feasible, and (if experience may add a word) merciful. They are not likely to set up an impossible standard of enforcement, one that would cause too rapid or too ruinous a dislocation; and for the same reason, when enforcement becomes necessary, they are likely to give it their full support. It is difficult to convey to amateurs in this field the extent to which the whole meaning and effect of legislation of this type depends on the knowledge, the tact, and the moral support of the inspectorate.

It must be remembered that, even under a labor government in England, there persists among trade-unionists a strong sense of caution about invoking the coercive powers of the state too lightly or too broadly. There is even now very little desire that the general level of wages should be state determined (despite the popularity of the benefit aspects of the Beveridge plan). There is evident in American discussion of minimum wage law a tendency to assume that legislation can, and perhaps should, raise the *general* level of wages. In so far as this assumption prevails, an impossible enforcement situation may be set up. The Fair Labor Standards Act of 1938 carefully enunciated a sound basis of policy; namely, that the elimination of oppressive or subminimal conditions was in the interests of the entire community. On that ground the Supreme Court was justified in stretching the Constitution to cover it. But in application of the principle, the Congress sanctioned two modes of procedure one of which is definitely unsound, and the other debatable.

It is an unsound procedure that statute law should embody specific figures of remuneration or of any other price. Reference may be made here to the particular rates of "fair return" specified in the Transportation Act of 1920 and the subsequent history of that provision. Conditions change too rapidly and too unpredictably for actual percentages, or dollars-and-cents specifications, to be incorporated in statute law. The authority of statute law should be reserved for the *principle* of action, clearly and judicially defined, leaving the application of the principle to administrative interpretation in the light of current conditions, subject to review.

Second, there is the question of the national flat-rate minimum. If the legislature wishes to proceed on this basis, it is obvious that its figuring will be of the rough-and-ready kind. We can argue the difference between seventy-five cents and a dollar an hour, but we can hardly argue whether 72 or 81 or 96 or 104 would be better, because the figure is mostly guesswork anyway. The wider the area of application, and the less discrimination there is between regions, trades, and industries, the more necessary it becomes to lean toward the lower limit of the rough estimate; because more damage and difficulty will result from the attempt to enforce in certain areas or occupations a figure that is too high for them than will result from tolerating in other cases a figure that is not so high as it might be. This follows inevitably from the flat-rate principle.

There is some reason to think that the upward pressure exerted by certain organizations springs from a desire to use the force of legislation to raise the *general* level of wages. Since current procedure throws the determination of the minimum figure into the arena of politics, that is hardly surprising; but the method is unsound and, in the end, unworkable. The same caution must be urged upon the administration of the Walsh-Healy (Public Contracts) Act. Apart from all economic arguments, there is the political consideration that it is far easier to expand than to contract. If a time should come when the statutory minimum needed downward adjustment, a very difficult situation might arise that moderation and foresight could forestall.

The surest guide to sound policy, in this and other cases that cannot here be argued, is a clear grasp of the moral principle involved. The basis of minimum wage law is to protect the good employer from the bad one; to protect those workers who are unable to protect themselves; and, in so doing, to make effective the moral consensus of the whole community. Whatever the means employed, freedom will be preserved just so long as the nature of the end is clear and no longer.

The tenor of the foregoing arguments will seem restrictive only to those who weigh lightly the prospect of increasing coercion against the benefits it is supposed to insure. The thesis here advanced is that even were those benefits general and certain—which they are not—the price would still be too high. But this thesis must by no means be taken to exclude the state, as one agency among others, from the execution of our common aims and purposes. What should be attempted, and how and when, are matters for practical realistic consideration; and there are many in which public authority may properly be used to the ennoblement of both itself and the community for which it acts. The criterion is simply the ground and the degree of coercion. Where the ends in view are such as to evoke general moral support, and public authority is evidently the best way to attain them, coercion will be at a minimum and no a priori objection will lie. In such cases legal compulsion will be applied only to situations that informed public opinion spontaneously condemns; it will be invoked only as a last resort; it will be generally supported when it is invoked; and it will therefore entail no general restriction on freedom.

Radically different is the policy which would use the coercive power to alter the normal workings of the voluntary economic system, for it shifts the ground of coercion. I am well aware that the term "voluntary economic system" cannot be interpreted in the twentieth century as simply as it was in the nineteenth; we shall have to re-examine its meaning. In so doing, we shall willingly recognize that the theoretical or programmatic basis of coercion may offer an admirable pattern of desirable ends. The products and social consequences of the free-enterprise system, especially in America, are far from ideal, and the present writer has frequently and specifically said so. It is not at all difficult to devise on paper a better layout of products and social situations, and many people find their satisfaction in doing so. That is not enough. The real problem is how to get from here to there. In practice, the means control the ends more powerfully than the ends control the means. A merely theoretical or programmatic basis of coercion, fully warranted as it may be by its own ideals and assumptions, may in execution so modify the character of the society that the ends themselves turn out to be quite different, on attainment, from what was originally intended. The policy, so to speak, tends to run away with itself. That is the danger against which any free people must be perpetually on guard.

VIII

COMMUTATIVE JUSTICE IN ACTION

✲

THE goal of commutative justice is equality. Not egalitarianism, which seeks to flatten out, usually by force, the natural diversities of endowment, heredity, aptitude, and luck; not even equality of opportunity, though that is an inseparable part of the general aim; but moral equality. It protects a man's right "to live a human life, to perfect his moral nature, to be treated as a free, intelligent, responsible human being." Its practical rule is the familiar "do as you would be done by," which, when Christianity started applying it without exception to all sorts and conditions of men, turned out to be a radically progressive principle. This is the rule of reciprocity, without which neither democracy nor economic freedom can be maintained. Beyond all considerations of class or caste, status, power, or privilege, this rule asserts the moral identity of rights and obligations which alone makes free community possible. As a revolutionary principle, this is perennial. We find it in the oldest and most persistent economic teaching of the Bible—the denunciation of usury. Hilaire Belloc, in one of his best papers, points out that an interest rate of 100 per cent may not be usurious, while a rate of 6 per cent may be.[1] The criterion is not the rate but the unconditional enforcement of interest on an unproductive loan. Westerners have no idea of what lies behind this, though they got a hint in some of the farm-mortgage auctions of 1932–33, where not a man present would make a bid (a bid meaning that a distressed farmer could be driven off his land). Outside the Western world, from

1. *Essays of a Catholic* (New York: Macmillan Co., 1931), Essay II.

Egypt to Manchuria, such familiar phrases as "sow in tears" and "cast thy bread upon the waters" had, and still have, a terribly poignant meaning. In a poor year the small farmer may have to starve his family in order to sow his next year's crop. He may have to resort to the moneylender. Come a second or a third bad year, and he is sunk; he may have to pledge his land, his daughters, his wife, and finally himself. This was what led to the Jewish institution of the sabbatical year (the seventh). It evoked the early Greek and Babylonian legislation dealing with the situation. And in Christian law the same situation still regulates the charges of those most useful social functionaries, the pawnbroker and the small loans corporation.

The underlying principle is so simple that there can be no argument about it: it is wrong for the wealthy person to take advantage of the need of the needy borrower. It took a long time to get this principle extended beyond tribal or racial boundaries. It took still longer to get it broadened and deepened into modern form. The commercial market for the supply and demand of investment funds had to be organized and distinguished, and that took most of the seventeenth and eighteenth centuries. False analogies like that of the biological struggle for survival got in the way. But finally the underlying principle reasserted itself, because it is essential to the growth of free community: it is wrong for the economically stronger to impose their will on the economically weaker. Economic conduct does not transpire in a moral vacuum; man does not live by bread alone.

This is far from meaning that economic conduct can be guided simply by wishes, aspirations, or ideals. There are facts to be reckoned with. When business and ethics are discussed as separate spheres or categories of conduct, economists as well as manufacturers are likely to take the cue and insist that "business is business." American businessmen are remarkably tolerant of sermons from all sorts of sources, and, like old-style British labor leaders, they preach some pretty good ones themselves—but not at directors' meetings. There, they feel, is a different universe of discourse—a very complex universe of fact that has to be dealt with on its own terms at the risk of total failure, a universe that is not amenable to sermons. Lord Josiah Stamp, whose death in the blitz was a major disaster for the Germans as well as the English, took an active interest in the relation of ethics to business. Good Christian that he was, he gave to it some of his best work and keenest thought. But he had very little use for sermons. Just as you live in a physical world, he would say, and have to reckon with its imperatives, so you live in an economic world and must pay attention to its laws. If you do not, so much the worse not merely for you but for the bit of practical good you might have accomplished. If or when (in 1926 he said "when") the general quality of human conduct is spiritually elevated over a wide enough area, then business motives may be sufficiently modified to alter the economic postulates. But in the meantime "what is economically sensible and feasible becomes an integral part of what is ethical, and is not rival or antithetic to something which we have independently determined as ethical."[2]

That did not mean, of course, that anything which business finds expedient or profitable to do in the short run has an intrinsic ethical sanction. It did mean, emphatically, that the efficient conduct of the world's work is a sounder basis for an ethical system than any amount of talk; for it is common work, rather than talk, that extends and deepens the areas of dynamic community. Stamp set a high *moral* value on economic realism. He thoroughly approved Comte's maxim that it is for the heart to suggest our problems and for the intellect

2. Josiah Stamp, *The Christian Ethic as an Economic Factor* (London: Epworth Press, 1926), p. 32.

to solve them. He urged "Christian enthusiasts, desiring to remodel economic society, to devote a little less effort to the elaboration of Christian principles and a little more to the patient analysis and study of underlying economic principles." Surely that was, and is, good advice for all enthusiasts. He added a characteristic aphorism: "Faith is more likely to move mountains if a whole multitude are also shoving, and shoving along the lines of geological least resistance."[3]

It followed, and Lord Stamp went to a lot of trouble to prove it, that even from the "proletarian" point of view, the efficiency of production was infinitely more important than the quarrel about distribution. British experience since he wrote amply confirms his judgment; American experience soon will. It also followed that in all disputes about fairness there could be, and should be, a considerable area of objective agreement as to the economic consequences of rival claims and policies. That area being impartially defined, there would then remain a zone within which ethical principles as such could be debated and applied.

But even within that zone we are not left to purely subjective interpretations of commutative justice. There are signposts, compass points, fundamental principles. One of them has just been mentioned; namely, that economic strength alone does not justify its possessor in imposing his will on others. Here and there, even yet, one comes across exponents of pseudo-Darwinian theories who talk and try to act as if it did. The atavistic strain in human nature, which Catholics quaintly call original sin, is always a fact to be reckoned with; but so is its antidote, the communal impulse that lies at the root of natural law. We shall never finally resolve this tension; or, if we do, we shall no longer be human.[4] The important

3. *Ibid.*, pp. 55–56. The book is rare and practically unobtainable; I cite it in tribute to a great and good man, untimely killed by total war.

4. Geometrical analogies have been popular since at least the time of Pythagoras. They have a suggestive value for certain minds beyond that of verbal or syllogistic

hing is to recognize it in its current forms and try to resolve t in current terms, for by that very effort we qualify ourselves or a higher degree of spontaneous community. Such effort is ssentially an adventure in mutual education, and American usiness organizations and service clubs deserve a lot more redit than they get for pushing ahead with it according to heir lights.

The medieval jurists and theologians have left us a carefully onsidered body of doctrine dealing with the concept of fairness. The care with which they considered it was natural and necessary, since they thought of economic conduct as merely a part of conduct in general, subject to the same principles of ustice and righteousness as applied elsewhere. Later centuries, dominated by a growing materialism, came to conceive of economic conduct as taking place all by itself in an ethical vacuum and developing its own "laws" or "forces" which neither could be nor should be interfered with. This notion has landed the modern world in a sorry mess, and we might well go back to the thirteenth century for a fresh start. Of course circumstances have changed since then, but we must beware of supposing that, because circumstances have changed, the principles of righteousness and justice have changed too.

From the work of our predecessors in the field of commutative justice we may pick up a couple of clues to the tangled situation of today. One traces the right relation between

---

logic. Nearly all are based on the triangle. Here is a modern example: imagine an equilateral triangle standing on its apex. The left radial (1) is thesis. The horizontal member (2) is antithesis—that is, the limiting conditions imposed as it were by the amorphous irrational outside. Subtending the angle is the right radial (3), the synthesis. The synthesis (3) now becomes the new (1) thesis; that is, the progression is lifted up a step. Again, at the outside angle, a new (2) is imposed; subtending this, the horizontal radial becomes a new (3) synthesis, which now becomes a new (1). So we go round the hexagon and discover that our original starting point (1) was itself at some time a (3) synthesis; that is, we realize that we are moving in a three-dimensional spiral. Of course this is no more than a parable, and equally of course, it is not limited to the three sensual dimensions.

sellers and buyers; the other the right relation between th
functional groups involved in the productive process. In nei
ther case shall we expect finality, in the sense of an *ipse dixit*
this is the sphere in which we are charged to work out ou
own salvation. But we shall find in the traditional teaching a
superior realism, inasmuch as the economic questions are deal
with from the moral angle, which is the one that ordinary
people naturally comprehend.

Among the pages of the canon from which we may stil
derive instruction is a very early one of Thomas Aquinas defining the essential condition of fairness in a bargain. The condition is equality of burden or sacrifice. What A offers to B should represent about the same sacrifice to A as what B offers represents to B. They both stand to gain from the transaction, each giving what he desires less in exchange for what he desires more; and Aquinas is careful to point out that they may gain unequally. "If a man is greatly aided by something he has gained from another, and the seller does not suffer any loss from doing without it, he ought not to charge more for it, since the advantage which accrues to the other is not due to the seller but to the condition of the buyer." There is a logic in that which becomes evident in those fourteenth-century statutes forbidding the artisans to take advantage of the scarcity of labor created by the bubonic plague; but since goods, including the necessaries of life, were also scarce and dear, there arose a renewed emphasis on fairness in pricing and marketing. The ancient laws against forestalling, engrossing, and regrating express the public resentment against attempts to create an artificial scarcity for the selfish benefit of one party; so does the common-law animus against restraint of trade, before which even Queen Elizabeth, granting patents (monopolies) to court favorites, had to bow. An illustration worth pondering today is the case of an Essex farmer who in 1631 held his grain off a rising market and was condemned

to pay 100 marks fine to the king, and 10 pounds to the poor, and to stand upon the pillory in Newgate Market an hour with a paper, wherein the cause of his standing there was to be written, put upon his hat, "For enhancing the price of corn"; and then to be led through Cheapside to Leadenhall Market, and there likewise to stand upon the pillory, and after this to be sent to Chelmsford, and there likewise.

That farmer was obviously a smart businessman and a good economist; but it was not enough. There is one aspect of his case to which we shall return: he was condemned, not for unfair competition, but for unfair conduct. His judges were not interested in competition as an automatic dispenser of justice. He might have been the only farmer in Essex, or in England for that matter; the sole effect would have been to get him a still stiffer sentence because of his greater responsibility.

The United States has accumulated a remarkable collection of laws, court decisions, administrative orders, and even newspaper advertisements about "fairness"—fair labor standards, fair employment practices, fair bargaining, fair wages, fair working conditions, fair return, fair valuation, fair trade (which means private price-fixing), fair competition (which damns it)—and now we have the "Fair Deal," whatever that may turn out to be. The point to notice is not the excellence of all these objectives but that the criterion is ethical, not economic.

Economics can arrange facts, analyze data, and often give a good forecast as to the results of alternative determinations; but, to decide which of them will be "fair," we must resort to other than economic considerations. The history of American railroad regulation shows conclusively that we cannot fix fairness by formula. After more than thirty years of trying, both the courts and the Congress were compelled to fall back on another batch of purely ethical terms such as "honest," "reasonable," "just," "prudent," etc. The record shows, in this and other cases (coal-mining in particular), a striking instability in the interpretation of such terms, including the term "fair" itself. Differences of opinion are of course natural and desirable so long as they acknowledge, or imply, a common ethos in the commonweal; but if, or when, they imply that justice itself is mere matter of opinion, then freedom of action for everyone and every group is in jeopardy. The danger to freedom arises not so much from the ambitions of power-hungry bureaucrats (of whom there are fewer in America than in most other countries) or from theoreticians in control of the Executive (even they have their disagreements). The trouble has a more practical origin.

When the various interest groups in the community are no longer in agreement as to the fundamental principles; when there is no common consensus as to the nature of commutative justice, or fairness, underlying their normal contentions; then they either resort to private coercion or throw more and more of their disagreements into the lap of the courts and the legislatures, demanding a coercive settlement of the disputed issues. But there is no reason, in a democratic society, to expect more fundamental agreement on that level than there was on the other; yet decisions have to be made. The result is naturally split parties and split verdicts. From either a labor or a business point of view there is no greater restriction on freedom of action than the uncertainty as to what is or is not allowable that is thus engendered. But the root of the trouble lies on the original plane. That is why—whether or not the particular arguments of this and comparable books commend themselves to the reader—discussion of the fundamental principles is of immense practical importance.

The Federal Trade Commission Act of 1914, as most readers will recall, is designed to prevent unfair methods of competition. When the bill was in the Senate, several members argued that some definition of the terms "fair" and "unfair" ought to go in; and there were some interesting suggestions. One of the most interesting was that "unfair competition" should cover practices for which the injured party could get redress only by going to law. In the end no definitions were inserted, very fortunately, as it turned out. Had definitions been laid down, business could always have kept one jump ahead of that particular game. Instead, business was presently required to draw up its own rules, as the broadcasting business is doing now; and though the rules may not be all that critics might desire, it is, I submit, better to have a high degree of voluntary adherence to a less perfect system than a high degree of legal coercion attempting to impose a more perfect system. For the sense of fairness is essentially a growing thing. Not only does it adapt its expression to changing circumstances; but it grows intensively, in the sense that practices that would have been freely tolerated in the 1890's would not be freely tolerated now. I am convinced that there has been in our time a much greater advance in voluntary business ethics than business generally gets credit for. (Why is it that one cannot say the same for international conduct?) Some of that advance, no doubt, is due to state action; but we do not behave like human beings simply from fear of the policeman. If fear of the policeman is all that stands between us and perdition, then we are lost already.

If I may continue for a moment to use the work of the Trade Commission as a text, there was one respect in which the law called for amendment. Fairness, I have suggested, is a moral quality of action that grows intensively in a free community. That is really an assertion of classical natural-law doctrine. Aristotle, we may recall, thought that there was "a certain natural and universal right and wrong which all men divine, even if they have no intercourse or covenant with each other." Similarly, according to Cicero, "nature ordains that one man shall desire to promote the interests of a fellow man, whoever he may be, just because he is a fellow man." Is that true? I think well enough of humanity to hold that there is some truth in it, but too abstract a truth to be of much practical service. But it is both true and useful within certain limits; namely, within those limits in which social life and common effort are facts of everyday experience rather than abstractions that have to be talked about.

That is one of the great arguments for decentralization. The small community does develop a strong sense of fairness among its members, which it implements without much resort to legal coercion. But there is often a difficulty in getting that sense applied to those who are not familiars of the community. In the sphere of "unfair methods of competition" the years—and the radio—brought an increasing number of cases in which certain practices (of misbranding goods, for example) injured no competitor, because the competitors knew too much to be fooled. The consumers were the ones who were fooled, and the law had to be amended to get them into the picture by adding the phrase "deceptive acts or practices in commerce." I mention the matter to suggest that special effort is and always will be needed for the continuous development of the moral consensus on which the freedom of any community depends.

In most ordinary situations of life we can and do rely on a common sense of fairness governing our mutual relations and transactions. We do not need laws and commissions to tell us that it is wrong to put sand in the sugar or water in the milk (or the stock). The protective devices we establish deal on the whole with exceptional cases. They include both official agencies and voluntary organizations such as the Better Business Bureaus of the larger cities. They try to insure that all parties may know the facts, especially in cases where the facts may be hard to obtain or be deliberately concealed, and that shysters are suitably discouraged. In this work, whether they know it or not, they are carrying on the great tradition of Christian ethics. Thomas Aquinas, for instance, deals with the delicate question whether a seller must reveal to the buyer defects in his goods—probably he had had some experience of traveling peddlers, since the resident merchant can seldom get away with it. Yes, says Thomas, he must; because if he does not, the buyer does not know what he is being offered; therefore equality of sacrifice will not obtain, and the bargain will not be fair. The rule was implemented not only by guild certification but by the appointment where necessary of state officials like the king's aulnager, whose duty it was to certify how much cloth there really was in the bolt. We do the same thing through such public inspectorates as those of the Pure Food and Drug acts—an excellent example of state enterprise, since it shows the state in pursuance of its cardinal aim, justice.

Our regulatory commissions, public or voluntary, often do more than that. They assist in focusing, making specific, the ideal of fairness as it applies to particular groups, trades, or industries. This policy as it was developed under Presidents Coolidge and Hoover tended toward the decentralization of power and the encouragement of vocational autonomy. The ensuing regime showed no such confidence in the voluntaristic principle. Its undoubted idealism took on an impatient, indeed an irascible, character, which boded ill for voluntary effort; and one of the results was the invocation of state coercion in spheres to which it was not appropriate and in which it could accomplish no abiding result. One of these was the sphere of employer-employee relations.

The medieval disapproval of collective action by employees —journeymen or apprentices—was based on the assumption that the employer, the guild, and the state accepted a positive responsibility for the maintenance of just wages and working conditions, so that private interference constituted an interruption of right order. With the breakdown and final abandonment of this system, the case for freedom of association could no longer be denied—as Adam Smith foresaw. Collective action became a necessary approach to equality of bargaining power by people who now had no reserves, no property, and no protection.

The right of association thus rests on a firm foundation of commutative justice; but it also raises new and largely unsolved problems because of the fact that private association obviously brings possibilities of private coercion far beyond what isolated individuals could exercise. These problems in their legal aspect go under the technical term of "conspiracy." This has nothing to do with treason trials and witch hunts; it refers to the fact that actions done individually may take on a different character and effect, for better or worse, when they are done in concert. If I decide to go jaywalking in our local Main Street, I may get killed by it, but I cannot (as yet) be imprisoned for it. But if fifty of us do the same thing together, we shall be obstructing the traffic, and the police will certainly have something to say.

It is unnecessary to list the varieties of labor action, or any other sort of collective action, on which this has a bearing; the point to notice is that the doctrine of conspiracy (to give it the bad old name) rests on fact, not theory. The British Parliament twice tried to deny this, with the intention of protecting trade-unionism from the assaults of an individualistic legal tradition. In 1875 it declared that no action done in furtherance of a trade dispute was punishable as conspiracy unless the same action were so liable when done individually. The Act of 1906

> explicitly declares, without any qualification or exception, that no civil action shall be entertained against a trade union in respect of any wrongful act committed by or on behalf of the union; an extraordinary and unlimited immunity, however great may be the

damage caused, and however unwarranted the act, which most lawyers, as well as all employers, regard as nothing less than monstrous. Trade unionists would be well advised not to presume too far on this apparently absolute immunity from legal proceedings.

That is the judgment of those famous arch-conservatives, Sidney and Beatrice Webb![5]

Their warning was insufficiently heeded; and the result, following the great strike twenty years later, was the Trade Disputes Act of 1927: a measure that corresponds in many respects to the American Taft-Hartley Act of 1947. Both were reactions against an excessive immunity conferred by law on what was supposed to be the weaker side; neither completely restored the balance. The British act outlawed strikes called for any other purpose than "furtherance of a trade dispute within the trade or industry in which the strikers are engaged"; in all other cases trade-union funds and officials were exposed to suit for injunctions, damages, and penalties.

The extremes of this measure have of course been modified, though no collectivist government is ever likely to restore to the unions their old autonomy—or irresponsibility, as authoritarians of both the left and the right would call it. But the point to notice about this British law is its premise. That premise was the official contention that the great strike was an attempt to coerce the government by holding up the community.[6] It was a contention with which the present writer emphatically disagreed (one has to be emphatic to contest any thesis of Mr. Winston Churchill). But whether or not that particular contention was sound, the fact remains that group coercion beyond a certain limit will evoke countercoercion, and the state, as the repository of the collective coercive power, will eventually be drawn in on the side of the status

5. *History of Trade Unionism* (1920 ed.), p. 606.

6. For details see the excellent account in W. H. Crook, *The General Strike* (Chapel Hill: University of North Carolina Press, 1931).

quo—unless a revolutionary situation is intended. There is no guaranty that such state action will bring commutative justice any nearer; it is merely the end result of the process of partial coercion. Therefore it is better not to rely on that process.

Putting this in more positive form, we may say that the right of association necessarily entails the responsibilities of association; these are different from, and graver than, the responsibilities of individual action and may properly be enforced. If the right of association is to be used, not simply as a mode of collective bargaining, not merely to secure a fuller participation by labor in the responsibilities of management, but as a means of attack upon the economic system, then the system will necessarily defend itself.

It is safe to say that there are very few people within the American trade-unions, and fewer still outside, who really wish to abolish the free-enterprise system or imagine that they would be better off under some other system. But there are very considerable numbers, including many writers for the labor press, who think it proper to represent that system as an implacable struggle between irreconcilable interests, with no holds barred, no mutual obligations of fairness, honesty, and decency, no consideration of third parties, no political program on either side that rises above the level of group selfishness.

That is precisely the way in which the real enemies of the voluntary system wish to have it depicted. It is a false picture, and no service to labor is rendered by efforts to make it true; for if it ever became generally true, the consequences would be far more disastrous than anything the Taft-Hartley Act contemplated. It is a fair demand of a long-suffering community that the immense powers of organized labor, which the American government itself has actively fostered in the last fifteen years, shall be used with restraint, forbearance, and a sense of social responsibility and that this sense be duly inculcated in he rank and file. The extent to which coercive action can accomplish, or even contribute to, this end, is very limited; we ave here a conspicuous case of the overestimate of political ction. But it is worth recalling that during these fifteen years n which trade-unionism has not been altogether unsuccessful n wooing the White House (as Mr. Dan Tobin among others would admit), business has had to adjust itself to a deluge of ontrols and regulations. Once the honeymoon of NRA was terminated in a none-too-friendly divorce, there came a spate of legal and legislative restrictions that is not yet over—investigations and injunctions, cease-and-desist orders, discriminatory and double taxation, antitrust indictments that were tried in the newspapers by Department of Justice officials long before they reached the courts, the far-reaching powers of the Securities and Exchange Commission, the vast and unrealized concentration of control over private banking, credit, and investment operations by the federal government and by administrative rather than legislative expedients, the equally unpredictable controls of every aspect of foreign trade, and the allocation of raw materials at home. In view of all this, it is not up to labor to squeal too loudly if at long last it too is reminded of its social responsibilities.

There is a widely disseminated idea that, since wage-earners are relatively numerous, their interests coincide with those of consumers generally. The Roosevelts, in all good faith, seem to have accepted this idea. But it does not follow that the particular interests of organized labor are in fact those of the general body of consumers. Even consumers have to eat, and not all the activities of organized labor make it easier for them to do so. Professor Slichter, in his remarkably compact study of *The American Economy* (Harvard University Press, 1948), represents the free-enterprise system as passing into the control of an employees' system—which he calls, rather ambiguously, a "laboristic system"; but he is very careful not to identify that with a system based on the common good. In fact, no systen of government which plays favorites among the many inter ests seeking control of the state can possibly be an instrumen of the common good; and, if or when the political system o democracy leads any government, or any candidate, to play favorites, then the days of that system are numbered.

Again, the pseudo-scientism of the intellectuals still encour ages the idea, though in terms somewhat different from those of sixty years ago, that if we can only hit upon the right for mula, social justice will automatically result without our hav ing to make any personal effort to secure it. A useful corrective is offered by a contemporary Catholic sociologist:

> It is not business that must be moral, but the business man. The talk about social morality has very much obscured this very simple fact. We expect to moralize business and the economic order, and after this has been accomplished men will naturally become moral. This hope is futile. Morality is a question of the individual conscience. The economic order does not reform men, but men reform the economic order.[7]

Nonetheless, there are special problems of morality that arise from the nature of group action and cannot be solved along individualistic lines. The doctrine of conspiracy represents a legalistic approach to some of them. Concerted action naturally contains possibilities of coercion that are not present in individual action; and the problems that arise are both interesting and difficult. It is a grave mistake to assume that they can finally be solved by fiat, whether of the courts, the legislature, or the Executive. The sound line of procedure, and in the end the only one, is to argue them out in the light of full information and put up as patiently as may be with the delays and inconveniences of that process. If there is no underlying common ethos in the community, the deficiency cannot be made good by extending the scope of coercion.

7. C. P. Bruehl, *The Pope's Plan for Social Reconstruction* (New York: Devin-Adair Co., 1939), p. 6.

Let us glance at what is probably the most difficult of these problems—the question whether a legitimate organization in pursuit of legitimate objectives may directly or indirectly coerce individuals into membership. This concerns both the closed shop (only union members may be hired) and the union shop (join up within a stated period after hiring). For the affirmative it is argued that, since the approved union officially represents all workers, all workers should be members. In the absence of a general requirement, the union may gradually be weakened by the systematic hiring of nonmembers. Since all get the benefits of union action, all should support it. Since the collective contract covers all, all should be parties to it. This last contention has given the French jurists in particular a lot of exercise. On the one hand, French law has been much more meticulous than English or American about the legal status of the collective contract. It can be (*a*) made binding on all parties directly concerned; (*b*) extended to cover a whole industry, including the unorganized sections. On the other hand, French law, with its strongly individualistic tradition, has been no less concerned about the right of an individual not to join the union if he does not want to; and American tradition also shows a lively interest in independence. As most people know, the independence of the nonconformist in this situation is pretty much of a fiction unless it is specifically safeguarded; and, even then, safeguards sometimes amount only to words against muscles. Can one have it both ways? What price liberty—versus solidarity?

A side issue may be promptly disposed of, namely, the political one. I can see no valid reason why trade-unions should not support political action if they want to. I can see valid reason why they should not aspire to party organization; but the decision is up to them. The British Labour party started out in 1901 on an avowedly class basis, and it has always been, and still is, handicapped by that fact. A class basis of political organization is not a good foundation for any democratic government, and, when supreme responsibilities come along, it usually has to be abandoned. That however is fact rather than argument. The one principle most people would agree on is that political freedom must not be curtailed by union membership. If a member of, say, the Teamsters' Union feels that he is a rock-ribbed Republican or a loyal Dixiecrat, political life will be the poorer if he is prevented from supporting and expressing his convictions, just as it would be if a member of the house of Morgan were prevented from supporting Mr. Henry Wallace. In political freedom we all have an interest.

But what about economic freedom? Let me instance a case in which the issue is even more sharply focused than in that of the closed shop. The British Joint Industrial Councils were officially inaugurated by the Asquith government as an effort to foster self-government in industry. No legislation was needed. These councils consist of representatives of trade-unions and employers' associations (not individuals, because organization was encouraged on both sides) meeting regularly to consider terms of employment and anything else they feel competent to discuss. There are now about sixty of them, and they discuss, often in consultation with government, all kinds of matters affecting their interests.

Early in the history of this movement an important issue arose which was pressed by the pottery industry. That was not, quantitatively speaking, one of the best organized on either side; but, qualitatively speaking, the reputation of the Wedgwoods for liberal leadership carried great weight. The issue was this: the organized section of the industry (and of some others) could reach agreement on terms and conditions of employment that were mutually satisfactory; but voluntary observance of such agreement was made extremely difficult by the undercutting of the unorganized section, in which conditions were admittedly substandard. If the agreed terms were reasonable from the public point of view, why should not their execution be protected by making them legally binding on the whole industry?

This was the issue that had perplexed French jurists torn between the principles of solidarity and individual freedom. It was a recurrent headache to British Ministers of Labour, whose official statements in the House had a distinct (and not wholly accidental) flavor of evasion. How would the reader decide the issue? This is an analogous case to the closed-shop question, but a stronger one, because here the demand for a compulsory rule is pressed by both sides.

The case was conceded by the British government to the cotton industry, and enabling legislation passed, in 1934. The principle has since been applied, but with extreme caution, to a few other industries. There are counterconsiderations. For one thing, not all trade-unions want it. It automatically extends the hard-won gains of organization and joint action to those who have done nothing to earn them. Per contra, it may be that the "fringe" people are simply too weak to do anything; and this may be true of employers as well as employees. But in such case will not the enforcement of minimum, as distinct from standard, rates suffice to lift them to the point at which they can do something and eventually come up to scratch? That is still, on the whole, the official line; but it has to assume that voluntary standards can survive the interval.

Second, and more important: if the force of law is to be put behind the extension of voluntary agreements, the content and details of those agreements must be subject to official scrutiny *and veto*. Not all organizations on either side want that. There are cases in which industrial harmony rests on a common, though tacit, conspiracy to gouge the consumer and break the competitor. This was not the situation in the English potteries; but there have been enough authenticated instances of this sort, both sides of the water, to warrant a policy of extreme caution.

Applying this argument to the closed-shop issue, it follows

that if coercion is to be permitted in regard to union membership, then the requirements of membership, including rules of work, dues, and initiation fees, must be publicly approved and sanctioned, for otherwise the right to work is obtainable only at a price dictated by an irresponsible monopoly. There are enough examples in operation to remind us that monopoly in this field was a major cause of the French Revolution. In that case the monopolists were capitalists, but monopoly by any other name. . . . We must note, however, that in the British problem above cited, and in this American question, extortionate terms are not the general rule. Great harm is done by overemphasis on what are, after all, exceptional instances. In general, terms of employment on which organized employers and wage-earners agree are reasonable terms; and, in general, the trade-unionist gets good value for the dues he pays. The ultimate question is whether society as a whole gets good value.

If that question is answered in the affirmative, then democratic tradition assumes that the proper solution will win on its merits. That may take time, and the time will be a testing time; but it is better for all parties to take their time than to demand an extension of the coercive principle and of the economic rigidity that goes with it. The extension of coercion is never a short cut. If 100 per cent organization is the proper solution, society still has an interest in keeping it voluntary. The basic obligation of the wage-earner, as of everyone else, is to his productive rather than his acquisitive function; moral considerations apart, it is the sole source of his income.

But moral considerations, as Lord Stamp pointed out, are not apart. We may say, speaking economically, that the rising cost of industrial strife takes from the worker himself more than he can hope to gain by the resort to coercion. We may say, speaking morally, that he is seldom justified in refusing his services to the community merely in order to increase his own share of a limited total product. In either case, we are really saying the same thing. What is of cardinal importance from the standpoint of commutative justice is that, as outsiders, we should qualify ourselves to say something intelligently.

The various regulative agencies of which we spoke earlier in this chapter rely in much of their work on what is really a very old principle—that of the *communis estimatio*, the common estimate in informed opinion of what is about right for the particular case. The Elizabethan labor code, for instance, gives positive directions to the justices of the peace about "calling unto themselves such discreet and grave persons of the said county or city as they shall think meet, and conferring together." We have seen in recent industrial disputes a remarkable and welcome revival of this principle, evidenced by the wide circulation of briefs and arguments, and the resort to newspaper advertising by both sides seeking to present their respective cases at the bar of public opinion.

In ordinary disputes the *communis estimatio* is not so vague a thing as it sounds. People who have had experience of labor hearings—newspapermen in particular—know that it is not difficult, in the average case, for an outsider to form a pretty close estimate of what will be humanly fair in the given circumstances. The difficulty often arises from the degree of stubbornness displayed on either side, sometimes with the deliberate intention of forcing the other to use what coercive power it possesses and thereby get itself a black eye from the public or the administration. If in principle we condemn the resort to coercion, that surely implies that we also condemn the resort to provocation.

As a matter of fact, and I use the expression in its literal sense, the controlling framework of the economic system rests not solely on the supposedly "inexorable laws" mechanistically interpreted but on a deeply based common estimate of what is right and reasonable in the economic relations of the different groups and functionaries. Customary wage differentials, profit margins, interest rates, even depreciation allowances, represent not merely the resultants of an abstract triangle or polygon of market forces but a human compromise between desire and necessity. From this continuous compromise it is neither possible nor desirable to isolate the mechanistic and the human elements and treat them as if they had no relation to each other.

This does not mean that all is quiet on the western front. Far from it. It does not mean that the present system can count on a persistent basis of common consent. Far from it. It does mean that proposals for basic change are entitled to much more careful consideration from the leaders of public opinion than they generally get and that such leaders, if they will take the trouble (for the material is abundant), can guide the underlying moral consensus toward lines of advance that are both feasible and desirable. For that consensus is ultimately the controlling factor; and it is a sad fact that the people who are supposed to be experts on morals—the preachers—tend to fight shy of any clear statement or analysis: either because they feel incompetent or because they are afraid of offending somebody.

Let us take the dominant industrial issue of 1949 as an example of the role that informed public opinion might reasonably be expected to play in a free society: the question of wage-earners' pensions. It is a major issue involving a matter of principle, and all parties have taken pains to put their arguments before the public. The pressure brought by the CIO unions on the mass-production industries was undoubtedly encouraged by the earlier success of John L. Lewis in fighting the case for the miners. Mr. Lewis has been cast for the role of public villain ever since he opposed the foreign policy of Mr.

F. D. Roosevelt, and perhaps he has rather enjoyed playing it. There is no man who stands in higher esteem on both sides of his industry as a negotiator or who has contributed more to the philosophy of labor-capital relations. Here is a bit of it:

> We hold that the proper care of the human element in the mining industry or any other major industry should properly be charged to the cost of production and not assessed against the taxpayers as a whole. To that degree, we think it's a step in the direction of free government. It's contrary to the concept that the Government should do everything for its citizens. The industry should do it, and the commodity should bear the cost of it. . . . A coal company is prohibited by law from using a mule or any other draft animal to the point where it is incapacitated and then turning it out on the street to die; and yet, that is what the bituminous industry has been doing with its man power.[8]

It must be added—since public memory cannot be bothered with figures—that the immediate reference here is to the (successful) demand that a man who has worked not less than twenty years in the mines should, on reaching the age of sixty, be given a pension, from the industry, of the sum of one hundred dollars a month. Government social security benefits might bring this up to as much as a hundred and thirty. Admittedly, that is more than most teachers could hope to retire on at sixty; but teaching does not produce as many broken backs as coal-mining. In the steel case the union's original demand was for $125 a month at the age of sixty-five. This, it must be remembered, was asked for on a noncontributory basis,[9] which would make it tantamount to a substantial increase in labor cost; and no one could or did contend that wages in the industries affected were unduly low. The real

8. Reprinted from *U.S. News and World Report*, an independent weekly magazine on national and international affairs, published at Washington. Copyright 1948 United States News Publishing Corporation.

9. Contributory pension and group insurance systems are generally in operation.

point was one of moral principle, as is evident in Mr. Lewis' statement just quoted.

Addressing themselves to this point, both Mr. Voorhees of "big steel" and Mr. Randall of "little steel" raised the question whether the individual worker is now so far gone that he cannot be expected to take care of himself. Wages, it was argued, are so adjusted in a free economy that the steady worker can, and if he is prudent will, provide for his own life-history; and there are plenty of voluntary agencies that will help him to do so. The analogy between mules, materials, machines, and men, said Mr. Voorhees, is a false one: "Machines are not paid current wages which they can freely elect to spend or to save. U.S. Steel does not own its employees; they are free men . . . privileged beyond most people with opportunity to provide for their own Sunday periods if they so choose." Is it either economically or morally advisable to tack on to the market wage system a further stipulation, which must obviously be uniform and independent of market conditions, for contingencies that any sober and sensible worker can foresee and forestall? May there not be a deleterious effect on the worker himself arising from this tendency to take his personal responsibilities off his own shoulders?

That is certainly an arguable case. Up to about 1910 it would have had the support of an overwhelming majority of economists and moral philosophers; it still has the support of a very substantial proportion, quite possibly a majority. What has the other side to say? For present purposes we need not go into the argument about profits—their amount, their justification, their disposition, their economic function. Not that these questions are irrelevant but that they tend to reduce the issue to a tussle between mere grab-groups; and it is essentially, on both sides, more and better than that: it is a moral issue, a problem in commutative justice that we all can understand if we are sufficiently interested in the growth of community to give our minds to it. (It is worth noting that, whenever Mr. Lewis takes a stand that seems arbitrary, it is—at least in his eyes—on a moral ground. Mr. Lewis is not a Welshman for nothing.)

At this point, so far as concerns the economic issue, a discussion of profit-sharing would be in order. There are many such discussions available to the general reader. But profit-sharing morally involves loss-sharing; and there have been many years in which large numbers of concerns showed very heavy losses, in some cases ruinous to both owners and employees. Great damage has been done by popularization of the phrase "the profit system" when realism demanded the phrase "the profit-and-loss system." Over the years, tremendous profits must be balanced against tremendous losses.

Again, there is considerable confusion in the public mind between the idea of profit-sharing and that of employee stock ownership. It is better to keep these ideas apart. We are not concerned, in this particular issue, with the notion of proprietorship. If we were, we should have to discuss the advisability for the employee of putting his savings into the same source from which his current income is derived. Normally, where security is the aim, one does not do that. But the pension issue is simpler. Many of us have known private employers who liked to acknowledge length and fidelity of service by gold watches, or cash bonuses, or some such tangible expression—the writer knew one very well indeed. To call this paternalism is one of those plausible travesties of truth to which modern terminology is so well adapted. It was rather the expression of a mutuality of relationship, a tacit partnership, that had been built up through the years of work irrespective of any difference in function. And it had nothing to do with wages; it lay in a quite different category: a moral category. As if the wage-earner had invested something of himself, beyond his paid labor (however well paid), in the concern he worked for, or in, or with. That is the way the plain man feels about it when he says that it is "wrong" to lay off an elderly worker merely on account of his age without some compensation. He cannot justify his resentment on strictly economic grounds, which merely shows that strictly economic grounds (if they still exist) are subordinate to moral ones.

As a matter of fact, there are few employers who in practice defy the principle. Even corporate employers have generally acknowledged it in some degree; some of them in a large degree. There is a growing recognition that the equivalent of proprietorship for the wage-earner—his equivalent for the increment of good cultivation—is a certain measure of financial security. It must not be assumed, as matter of fact or of principle, that the directors of modern large-scale corporate enterprise are unaware of their moral responsibilities. It would be nearer the truth to say that society has assigned them the task of reconciling its demands with its moral consciousness. In that task it is necessary that the directors of both employees and investors work together; if they will do so with reasonable patience and objectivity, industry can adjust itself to rising ethical standards as it has repeatedly done before and with a diminishing instead of an increasing need for legislative or judicial coercion.

My intention in citing this illustration is not to argue the issue but simply to show that the issue is arguable by any informed layman who will take the trouble to think. One grows weary of the sort of American idealist who gets excited about the state of affairs in Manchuria or Indochina or the Dutch East Indies (as to which he or she really knows very little) and then, when you ask for his opinion on an issue cropping up in his own back yard, turns round and pleads incompetence. That is the attitude that gives the Communist his desired opportunity, for the Communists really do study these issues and study hard. There is no excuse for it. One of the dangers to a free and prosperous society lies in the tendency to invoke general phrases such as the "common good" or the "public welfare" and then leave somebody else to define and apply them while we all go about our own business and have as good a time as we can afford. It is entirely human and natural to do so; but we must remember that democracy is the most difficult form of government, demanding an exceptional degree of economic, political, and moral intelligence from its leaders. If that is not forthcoming, democracy will not work.

The European visitor, especially if he is British, German, or Scandinavian, is likely to be struck by the meagerness in both quantity and quality of adult education in America, especially by the paucity of the radio contribution. Even the book sales, despite the admirable enterprise of American publishers, are nothing to brag about when compared on a per capita basis with poverty-stricken Europe. The hectic, almost desperate hunt for entertainment suggests that Americans have either forgotten, or not yet discovered, the satisfaction that intellectual competence in some small field can give when it is earned—as, of course, it has to be. For those who will take a real interest in social and economic questions there is also a more tangible stake. The layman can contribute something toward industrial peace by trying to form his own opinion on the basic principle, for, though it would be too much to say that coercive methods cannot succeed when public opinion strongly disapproves their aim, they are at least *pro tanto* weakened and discouraged; while, when public opinion can be won round to a general approval, the case for moderation and deliberation is substantially strengthened.

One of the more promising movements toward a higher level of commutative justice is the effort many business firms are making—notably General Electric—to instruct and interest their employees in the current economic condition of their own concern. As we began by saying, ideals of justice lose their cogency if they are not rooted in economic realism. It is therefore a moral obligation on all who press for change to take the trouble to master the facts in the first place; indeed, we might well omit the qualifying clause. For the degree of solidarity between those who are actually engaged in the productive function is and should be greater than that obtaining between the absentee owners—the eight hundred thousand small stockholders of "Tel. & Tel.," for example—despite the legal fiction of ownership applying to the latter. The practical relationship of the producers to the multitude of investors is a fiduciary one; the relationship of the producers to one another is familial or at least functional. The former relationship must be scrupulously honored; it is based on good faith and confidence, and on its observance depends the supply of capital for the maintenance and development of the voluntary economy. If it is not so honored, the state will invoke its coercive power to fulfil that function.[10] But the relation between the producers and the investors does not necessarily dominate the relation between the different groups of functionaries, as some would have us believe. The former acts as a limiting condition on the latter, but the limits are wider than is generally supposed. After all, the average investor is not less interested in security than is the average wage-earner and not less entitled to it. Within the limits thus set, however, there are wide possibilities for the development of functional solidarity. These possibilities are impeded equally by irresponsible demands of either investors or employees for an increase in their respective shares of the joint product. It is high time we outgrew that stage of conflict.

10. The British National Transportation Board has just announced a loss of four and three-quarters million pounds for the year 1948, with a heavier loss in prospect for 1949; it adds that railroad equipment is still antiquated. The sole alternative to obsolescence is more taxation.

We shall not outgrow the conflict itself. In czarist Russia as in socialist Britain there is still the struggle between the legitimate demand for more capital and the desire for more consumer spending; it may quite possibly break both systems. We in America are not exempt from it, as any businessman will testify. Our peculiar challenge is to find an answer to it that is consistent with the maintenance of a voluntary economic system. So far no extant society has found that answer. The usual resort is to increasing state coercion, which, if history has any meaning, is no answer. National states are not the spokesmen of God Almighty; or, if they are, our conception of the deity is a total illusion. The solution, if there is one, is up to us—a challenge to human intelligence and good will—and it would be less than fair to the reader if the implications of what has already been said were not fully exposed in their relation to certain popular American stereotypes.

IX

COMPETITION OR CONTROL?

☼

IN THIS and the final chapter I shall try to indicate, and briefly to illustrate, some of the underlying tensions or issues into which our historic situation is now propelling us. Such matters are not easily outlined, even roughly, because in the nature of the case we are not yet fully aware or conscious of them. But, as I have repeatedly urged, it is both our interest and our obligation to achieve as much advance awareness as we can, so that we are not continually being taken by surprise at the turn of events. This chapter will deal mainly with the domestic situation, the next with the external prospect. But the separation between these spheres becomes increasingly arbitrary and unrealistic, and that is the first and fundamental thing we have to recognize.

In both spheres the issues that confront our generation arise from the tension between the same three elements: the inherited structure of the modern closed societies, political, economic, and cultural; the pressure against this structure of applied science and technology, which is not only a material but an ideational pressure; and the universal impetus toward higher moral standards. This last manifests itself at present chiefly by way of advanced ideas as to what is due to a man as a producing member of any organized society, and it has an obvious relation to the second factor; but not, I would say, an exclusive relation (we may leave the sociologists to argue about that). In any case, it generates its drive on the moral plane as an increasing sense of solidarity; and our immediate problem is to keep the local solidarities from colliding once again and reinvoking the satanic principle of force to the uttermost; secondarily, to keep our own solidarity, and what others we can influence, on a basis of voluntary action and personal freedom. Oddly enough, this is what the Marxists want too, if we may judge by their official texts; and it will help to clarify the present thesis if we take a preliminary look at Marxist eschatology.

The feature of it that naturally interests all liberals is its doctrine of the "withering-away" of the state; but that applies, we must remember, only to the state of the new, post-revolutionary world. To that article of the credo, one is tempted to say, all good Communists adhere—with the proviso that everything else must wither away first. But that is no worse a gloss than what most Christians put upon Christianity. Marx dreamed of a society so spontaneously co-operative that the need for general coercion would disappear. He masked his vision, and all but lost it, in a fabric of pseudo-science that has gone the way of other mechanistic philosophies; but it is fair to remember that Marx thought of the coercive, dictatorial stage as only temporary. Beyond it lay "the true realm of freedom" in which the creative spirit of man would develop its full powers; then real history would begin (what Communist societies have hitherto provided is presumably not a fair sample).

This apocalyptic vision of Marx is in the great tradition of the Old Testament prophets, inspired by a similar moral passion and compassion; but to him it seemed to indicate a very different consummation from theirs. We say "seemed," because it is possible, without straining the texts, to recognize in Marx so many of the elements of their Weltanschauung. Not only were the things they denounced the things he denounced—though, strictly interpreted, his theory gave no ground for denunciation—but the symbolic concepts reappear in thin disguise: the chosen people, chosen not to rule but to redeem; the innocent scapegoat, the suffering Son of Man, the supreme crisis (crux, crucifixion), the day of judgment, the triumph of the meek, the parousia, the new world in which the spirit of freedom will resume its pristine name of love. It is interesting, and not altogether futile, to speculate on what Marx might have become had not his father decided to make a little Protestant of him at the age of six, for the living core of his message sprang from the stem of Jesse.

But the *Zeitgeist*, whose native tongue is German, bade him be a dialectician; and the English, who usually interpret, helped to make him a materialist and an atheist. Marx admired Hobbes as a precursor in materialism, and the French kicked Hobbes out of court as "the father of atheists." How times do change! Just as Hobbes regarded his fellow-creatures merely as members of a species, Marx regarded them (for scientific purposes) merely as members of a class—we have his own word for it.[1] In both cases the materialist assumption required a merely quantitative view of social forces, as it necessarily and always does. Out of that could come nothing but a tyranny—a tyranny of the majority, perhaps, but nonetheless, or all the more, a tyranny. Thence arises the impossibility, today or ever, of reconciling the dictatorship of the proletariat, or the absolute monarchy, or "the party," or any other embodiment of absolutism, with the goal of freedom that Marx himself propounded. His premises doomed his system. Only his passion lives.

This radical incompatibility in the Marxist system between "scientific" (*scil.* materialistic) means and the ideal end is highly significant for modern liberals. Marx and his disciples,

1. Preface to the first edition of *Das Kapital*. See A. D. Lindsay, *Karl Marx's Capital* (London: Oxford University Press, 1925), chaps. i and ii, and cf. Max Eastman's Introduction to the "Modern Library" version of that work. The contrast between the two commentators is very instructive.

including Laski, see the state primarily as a coercive apparatus. That is why it is worth "capturing." In this view they are quite right. We shall run into all kinds of difficulty if we ever forget that the cardinal characteristic of the state, the attribute that distinguishes it from all other forms of association, is its monopoly of coercion. Neoliberals, in their devotion to good causes and worthy programs, tend to ignore this basic fact, or they take it for granted that the merit of their immediate ends more than offsets the coercive nature of the means.

Underlying this attitude are two ideas that are very generally confused but essentially in contrast. One is that of the state as standing above the democracy, accomplishing for the mass of the people various good ends that they are incapable of achieving without its instrumentality. Its mandate is usually assumed to be a majority, or a plurality, of the popular vote; but it can also be an organized minority (party, movement, *Bewegung*) whose mandate is derived from the alleged generality of its good intentions. This is, on the whole, the New Deal formula, not only in America but in England, France, and Germany. It is the utopia of planners and theorists, on whom the coercive aspect of state procedure makes little impression, since they do the coercing. Their excellent intentions are sufficient assurance that they will do it well and wisely; but the same justification points to an indefinite extension and prolongation of state activities.

The collection of people opposed to this program ranges all the way from Hilaire Belloc to Lenin. The radicalism of the extreme right agrees with that of the extreme left in wanting to eliminate the state rather than to enlarge it. The attack of the Chester-Belloc on the welfare (or "servile") state has a curious counterpart in the attack of the orthodox Marxists on reformism. Both attacks bogged down in what was really the same swamp; the former got lost in a romantic nationalism, and the latter ended up in the New Economic Policy. In both cases there were survivors plodding their separate ways through the waste land; and it is permissible to dream of a better world in which Dorothy Day and Leon Trotsky smoke the pipe of peace around the same fire.

There is an exciting resemblance between the goals of both Christian and anti-Christian revolutionaries. Both, in their several ways, pray the ancient prayer for the coming of the kingdom. Both agree that citizenship will rest on spontaneous fraternity. All talk of "rights" will cease; each will contribute all he can and take what he needs, and no one will have "to calculate, with the hard heartedness of a Shylock, whether he has not worked half-an-hour more than another." It is cheap and easy, continues a modern prophet,[2] to sneer at all this as merely utopian. True, "we cannot know" just when or how the new society will come; the materials for such knowledge are not available to us; and there are times when we "suffer to the point of torture" from the sense of our own inadequacy. But "progress marches onward"—obviously, in the light of faith. From both Christian and anti-Christian camps men and women have willingly gone forth to sacrifice their lives for their faith. In one camp only is it forbidden to sacrifice the lives of others.

And there lies the difference. The wings of vision that sustain the modern Communists are clipped by their own dogma. Stuck fast in nineteenth-century materialism, they never get off the ground. "Natura non facit saltum," they chant in melancholy chorus, unable to admit that that is precisely the reason why, at the human level, supernature steps in. Dreaming of a society only a little lower than the angels, they construct one only a little higher than the brutes because that is the utmost their materials will allow them. Their sacred texts

2. Lenin, *State and Revolution* and *What Is To Be Done?* reprinted in Columbia University Press, *Source Book on Contemporary Civilization* (New York, 1946), Vol. II.

are full of Darwinism, evolutionism, scientism, quantification, lifted out of proper context and applied to history and society in a fashion that begs the question of human nature at the very outset. Their extreme abstraction or generality serves a double function: it carries the requisite emotional charge and at the same time proffers a specious objectivity that is insulated from both fact and personality. It offers a system of propositions that might be true of things or animals as the sole basis for dealing with human beings. The Marxist "class" bears more resemblance to an animal herd than to any identifiable human solidarity, though even so the herd has more reality; but, whereas your dog is none the worse if you count on his herd instinct, infinite harm is done to human beings by denigrating them to that degree.

Here is a sample of what this leads to in the way of policy, a straight paragraph from Lenin's *State and Revolution*. Notice in it the following characteristics: the abstraction of the concepts, the immediate connection of these abstractions with force, the mechanistic or subhuman conception of the force, the associated passion, the scarce-concealed contempt for the masses—the writer knows very well that the term "militia" is itself a demand for military obedience. But remember also that Lenin was no more of a brute than you or I. In point of personal virtue he would rate higher than most of us. H. G. Wells, to his own surprise, could not refrain from describing him as a "very great man." He was a cultured and essentially kind person, appreciating the arts and amenities of life no less than we do, but never forgetting, as Trotsky says of him, "that as yet these things are the property of a small minority." We can hardly reproach him with that. Now listen to him as theorist and prophet:

Democracy is a form of the state—one of its varieties. Consequently, like every state, it consists in organised, systematic application of force against human beings. This on the one hand. On the other hand, however, it signifies the formal recognition of the equality of all citizens, the equal right of all to determine the structure and administration of the state. This, in turn, is connected with the fact that, at a certain stage in the development of democracy, it first rallies the proletariat as a revolutionary class against capitalism, and gives it an opportunity to crush, to smash to bits, to wipe off the face of the earth the bourgeois state machinery—even its republican variety: the standing army, the police, and bureaucracy; then it substitutes for all this a *more* democratic, but still a state machinery in the shape of armed masses of workers, which becomes transformed into universal participation of the people in the militia.

It is to be noted, in this and all other modern Communist pronouncements, that the notion of the "withering-away of the state" applies not to the existing so-called "capitalist" state but to the proletarian state that is to come after it. The former has to be "smashed," and only force will do it. In mobilizing that force, as recent disclosures have illustrated, anything goes; there is, as we observed earlier, no limiting ethic that binds all men. The Kantian idea of universal obligation is frankly abandoned. Life is not sacred, and honor has only a cash value in the courts of the enemy.

Nor can justice exist as we innocently conceive it. Professor Laski, following the orthodox line, proclaims that "the essential purpose of the state is always to protect a given system of class relations." In our society, according to this thesis, the state is merely the executive organ of "that class which owns, or dominates the ownership of, the instruments of production."[3] How far the facts of modern American democracy bear this out may be left for the evidence to decide; we need only remark that, if this is true, the possibility of justice disappears from any society that is not completely and totally egalitarian. Even in such a case we must assume an extraordinary and spontaneous like-mindedness which would resemble that of a herd rather than a human community. Short

3. H. J. Laski, *The State* (New York: Viking Press, 1935), p. 293.

of that ideal the control of the state by any class, even the most numerous, affords no possibility of equal justice; the state is merely the instrument by which one class exploits another.

The members of the Supreme Court of the United States take an oath that is eloquent in its simplicity: "I will administer justice without respect to persons, and do equal right to the poor and to the rich." According to the Marxist evangel, that is impossible, because the foundations of such justice do not exist. Similarly, where the Constitution requires the American government, as the very first of its specific duties, "to establish justice," we learn that no such aim is attainable until the type of society that the Constitution recognizes has been "wiped off the face of the earth." All this from people who have shown themselves capable of heroic sacrifice, to the point of martyrdom, for an admirable ideal of spontaneous fellowship and brotherly love!

Whence this amazing paradox? Its obvious sources are the materialism and the biologism by which the grand scheme of Marx himself is dated. That particular issue is now hardly worth powder and shot. Even a century ago it cost Marx a considerable effort to solve the recurrent soul-body dilemma by the simple expedient of denying the soul; and there is room for doubt whether he was ever quite reconciled to the results of that castration. He protests too much; and both he and Engels got quite angry with people who called them economic determinists. Nowadays no educated person talks in terms of the old body-soul dichotomy. The Catholics always denied it by their stubborn insistence on the concreteness of the sacraments and their worship of a Person rather than a theory. It is far more reasonable to believe in miracles than to believe in brutes. But the Gestalt psychologists, the physicists, even the biologists and psychoanalysts, no longer regard dogmatic materialism as a live issue.

Its obsolescence, however, by no means solves the Communist paradox—on the contrary. The effort to cling to a pattern of action whose metaphysical foundations have dissolved encourages negative rather than positive emotion; and in difficult times there is always plenty of negative emotion (to give it a polite name) looking for a pretext. That is, analytically speaking, a minor matter. What is really tragic is the thwarting, or subversion, of the positive emotion. As to the ideal of human community, both Catholics and Communists can feel—even though they cannot think—together; but, when it comes to argument, their talk lies on two different planes. The Communist tradition looks for the "coming of the kingdom"—the realization of the true community—in the same time and space as that in which we catch trains, do our shopping, buy insurance, and work for a living. Christ never thought that or taught that: "My kingdom is not of this world." In it, yes, as Christ is in it; but not of it.

The Communist perspective lies on a two-dimensional plane to which (perhaps but I doubt it) the animals are confined; and on that plane, since the millennium also lies on it, we are excused for an interim resort to the methods of the brute. (No, the analogy breaks down; nothing in the animal world even approaches the cold diabolism of modern war—class war or national war; nothing whatever.) And because the materialist millennium is supposed to lie in this same time and space—there being none other—the authenticity, the significance, of the concrete here-and-now perpetually dissolves in the "incessant extermination of past by future."[4] Nothing in the present is firm or final. There are no binding rules, no absolute values; anything goes; everything is "relative" or "instrumental," because the only meaning assignable to the human struggle lies somewhere other than here and sometime other than now.

4. N. Berdyaev, *The Meaning of History* (New York: Charles Scribner's Sons, 1936), chap. x; see also my *Liberal Tradition*, chap. xi.

Yet here-and-now is where we live. Society is therefore reduced, not so much to a state of chronic crisis (which might have an issue), as to a state of chronic deliquescence; and the very people who tell us that this world's values are all there are deny us the possibility of enjoying them in our time, because our time is only a way station on the road to Klondike.

It is worth noting, parenthetically, that a similar paradox was reached and recognized, two generations ago, by the aesthetic hedonists. No one protested more eloquently against the "incessant extermination of past by future" than Walter Pater; no one more persuasively vindicated the values of the here-and-now; and no one more sincerely demonstrated the inadequacy of materialism to sustain precisely those values. Pater's greatest work, *Marius the Epicurean*, was written with this express intention. Fifteen years earlier, Ibsen had wrestled with the same problem in his heroic drama, *Emperor and Galilean*. Fifteen years later Merejkowski was giving us a further statement in his great trilogy. The literature of western Europe is dominated by this issue. It is depressing to observe how completely the American intellectual perspective has been foreshortened by its preoccupation with "current events." Nothing gets out of date so quickly as the up-to-date.

What escape is there but to add a new dimension to the defunct geometry of flatland? We have to learn, or relearn, to see our fellow-creatures in the solid, as flesh and blood like ourselves. How real and rambunctious are the personalities of medieval and Renaissance literature compared with the wan wraiths that haunt our modern poets! How much tougher is the fiber of thought and theory than that of the modern "isms" and "ologies"! Science plays a grim joke on all who bend the knee to it. Its methods of classification and quantification have both use and beauty within their proper sphere; but, when those methods govern the treatment of human beings, their natural effect is to reduce human beings to the status of scientific objects, mere digits in a class or group or nation. "It is illogical," says Ortega y Gasset, "to guillotine a prince and replace him by a principle. The latter, no less than the former, places life under an absolute autocracy."[5]

There are genuine advantages to be gained by treating human beings simply as scientific objects. They breed, eat, suffer epidemics like any other biological species, and biological treatment can attain valuable results. Whether their work cooperation is of the same order as that of ants, wasps, and beavers seems to be doubtful; there are awkward factors of will, intelligence, and even imagination that get in the way. The creatures, for instance, have often shown a propensity to build cathedrals when they should have been building houses or battleships; but scientific treatment may in time eliminate all that. Its superior efficiency is obvious, given proper organization. An army is a much more efficient organization than a free society. The latter has to put up with a lot of muddling, blundering, and downright sinning. An army has a shorter way. Since it is a coercive organization internally as well as externally, cross-purposes do not have to be tolerated. An army, being a completely planned society, can, if necessary, be run without any monetary system and does not have to bother with bargaining, collective or individual. The members of the military society are not required to discuss ends; their concern is simply with means, that is, with "efficiency." What could be more efficient than an electric trigger that will wipe out at a touch a hundred thousand human beings and all their works?

Let us therefore praise the great god Efficiency. All he demands is that we make straight his path through the desert and purge the opposition. Personal consideration must not be allowed to stand in the way. Should the bomber and the bomb-maker be required, as a part of their education, to ex-

5. *The Modern Theme* (New York: W. W. Norton Co., 1933), p. 35.

perience the receiving end of their activities—to see the children with their hands torn off, to smell the flesh burning onto their bones, to hear the screams of the not-yet-dead in the mounds of the ruined city? No, indeed! That might retranslate the abstract into the concrete, with results disastrous to the unity of our collective purpose. Sternly, righteously, and increasingly we must exclude the personal from our calculations. We are not really killing children—who would want to do that?—we are not really killing anybody: we are simply attacking "the enemy" or "liquidating the opposition." The bomber and the commissar graduate from the same school: good people, fine public servants and university presidents, devoted to their respective prescriptions for the coming of the kingdom, and utterly devoid, as of course they should be, of personal considerations.

Surely it is a legitimate pride in human efficiency that animates all these people. How much more mastery is evident in the controls of a supersonic plane than in the clumsy splendor of some medieval shrine! How much higher a peak of human achievement! Human? Let us not be too particular about that, for this is where science plays the joker. The pilot controls his wonderful machine by doing just what the machine requires. He achieves just what the machine is capable of achieving. In the end, for practical purposes, he becomes what the machine permits him to become—just that, no more. So do we all who intrust our concrete human ends to the operation of abstract inhuman means. We arrive at "justice" without mercy, "liberation" without liberty, "victory" without peace, "efficiency" without effect, "power" without potency—because the means we collectively employ lie on a plane so different from that of the ends we humanly desire that, the more they succeed, the more they fail. That is the nemesis of all "great powers" and of all who put their trust in them. God knows, this is not a new story.

What then? We have to act together; we have to do things in association; we are powerless otherwise. This very necessity, intelligently accepted, becomes the basis of true freedom and joyous community precisely because it is natural to us. The co-operative pursuit of valid ends is one of the deepest sources of human happiness.[6] Marx saw that and rightly insisted on it, as if, with a divine persistence, the Christian evangel had penetrated to the very heart of the anti-Christian eschatology. At what point then does the latter go wrong? What transforms a true and life-giving communism (if we may rescue the term from its captors) into a false and deadly collectivism? Obviously, it is the kind of thinking that is brought to bear. When the method of abstraction is made the basis of a system of coercion operating in a purely spatial time, the consequences are bound to be subhuman. If in the sphere of means you begin by eliminating personality, you will not be able to reinsert it at will in the sphere of ends; for the kind of ends which your means can compass will have no place for it. You may like to think, or dream, differently, as most American Communists do; but the actual evidence is overwhelming.

It is for this reason that free societies must always be cautious about the introduction into government of this kind of thinking. Abstraction, quantification, and coercion all belong together; and none can deny that there are tangible short-run results to which these methods are an effective short cut. In an army the individual person becomes merely a function with a number, and therein lies efficiency. There is a price to be paid for keeping community spontaneous all along the line, and sometimes it seems foolish to go on paying it. The ultimate question is what one wants out of life—not in Klondike, but here; not in the millennium, but now.

6. The work organization, and its results, at Trinity College Chapel, Hartford, Connecticut, or the Anglican cathedral at Liverpool, England, are outstanding modern illustrations; but one could also cite many a New England barn.

That is where the choice arises. Just because we confer on the state a monopoly of coercion we are tempted to invoke its coercive powers as a short cut, forgetting that our reason for giving the state a monopoly of coercion is to get rid of coercion. The state, properly conceived, is an instrument of freedom. The bases of its authority are moral, not material. What it enjoins upon us is that we act like human beings, in the better sense of the term. To that command we give a spontaneous assent, thereby enlarging, not diminishing, the scope of our freedom. As the instrument of a *moral* solidarity, there are no a priori limits to the organizing and directive functions that may be assigned to the state by the free community; but its coercive powers may not be invoked for any lesser end than that of a fuller humanity now. The distinction—which the remainder of this work will illustrate and apply—has been well put by Professor John Jewkes in his *Ordeal by Planning:*

> The most deep-rooted sickness of the planned economy is that it seeks to bind together the community by an appeal to an end which cannot provide any lasting social cohesion—the pursuit of wealth. It is ultimately disastrous to expect men to enjoy the communion of their common brotherhood, their sense of playing their part in some satisfying joint effort, their feeling of the unfolding of the full potentialities of their personality by putting before them a target (incidentally fixed by someone else) for the output of steel, coal, electrical switches or paper bags. . . . For the pursuit of wealth cannot bind men together, it is a centrifugal not a centripetal force. The vow of poverty can bring social cohesion. But not the vow of plenty. . . . In the last analysis the spiritual content of planning proves to be a sham.[7]

There are few among us who would consciously surrender, for any prize whatever, the ideal of spontaneous co-operation that is so vital a part of the "American way." Its harshest critics dream of more spontaneity even while they plan for

7. J. Jewkes, *Ordeal by Planning*, chap. xi. New York, 1948. Published by The Macmillan Company and used with their permission.

less. None would deny the amazing harvest it has yielded, not merely of goods and services but of men and women. Let no temporary confusion, no salutary disillusion, goad us to such impatience that we sell our birthright.

But merely to reaffirm the ideal of the voluntaristic, or personalistic, society solves no immediate practical problems. Instead, it makes them more difficult—or, at any rate, more profound. By disparaging resort to two-dimensional blueprint solutions, it consigns us to dig deeper in order to build higher, as is very evident in the passage just cited. In so doing, we encounter familiar problems at fundamental levels. One of these is the old problem of personal freedom—physical, mental, moral—within a highly integrated, economically motivated society.

Some of our finest people have been telling us for a long time that the problem is insoluble; that, unless or until the society is radically transformed, the only thing to do is to get out of it. Associated with this counsel we often find the dislike of "bigness" which animates many groups of people, from certain Roman and Anglo-Catholic reformers to some recent majorities of the Supreme Court, though one would hesitate to say that the motives were exactly the same in all cases! There is, however, a common moral basis. Part of it is the old maxim that it is wrong for the economically stronger to take advantage of the economically weaker. (In citing this rule in this connection, I am not implying that they always or necessarily do—a recent Supreme Court verdict turned on this implication.) But there is a deeper element; namely, that there are certain values, personal and social, inherent in the life of the "small man," assuming he is truly independent, that are worth preserving.

The ideal of the small independent craftsman or farmer has a universal appeal and an unqualified validity; but it is not an economic ideal. All the more for that reason would some of us defend it: Arthur Penty, Eric Gill, Wilhelm Röpke, and many American and British veterans of the two world wars who would rather run a small farm or shop or roadside stand on their own than become employees of even the most benevolent of corporations. More power to them! But I am convinced that *as a general principle* we cannot revert to small-scale ideals. Our own human abilities have disposed of that possibility. I am even more convinced, however, that within the basic framework of an intelligently devised world economy there will be more scope for choice of vocation, independent living, and freedom from coercion than there is now, and far more chance of intellectual, material, and spiritual peace. It is not for everyone (though it certainly is for some) to strive to isolate himself from our complex, exacting, but wonderfully productive economic society.[8] There is nothing inherently derogatory to human nature, nor detrimental to human freedom, in the status of wage employment. On the contrary, it is the one way in which those of us who neither want to be, nor are qualified to be, entrepreneurs can earn enough security to live our own lives. Sure, it imposes on us what Rexford Tugwell called, in a book of that name, *The Industrial Discipline;* sure, a good deal of the discipline is monotonous—ask any schoolteacher. All sustained work entails a lot of monotony; did the reader ever try to build a wall or paint a trellis? It is a matter of the spirit in which the work is done; that is—though we do not usually stop to think about it—of our sense of conviction as to the worth-whileness of the work, either to us personally or to the multitude of our fellow-creatures whom we

8. The teachings and example of Gandhi, even when they seemed to refer to economic life, were intended as *spiritual* teachings. It may be that our era, like other aging cultures, brings a revival of the eremetic impulse; there is a striking revival of the growth of religious communities. But their utmost efforts, which are very powerful, will not absolve those of us who are "in the world" from fatalism, indifference, or "accidie." On all Christian people, hope is a spiritual injunction, not a sentimental recommendation; and "the sins against hope are presumption and despair."

never see, never know, and never hear from.[9] The dominant impersonality of modern economic life is a psychological, not a material, phenomenon; and many of those who are most worried by it would profit by following a very simple rule of action: if you do not feel that what you do for a living is intrinsically and socially worth doing, get out and do something else, even if you make less money. You will be otherwise rewarded, and society will be the better for your decision.

But if no *general* line of advance is to be sought in a restoration of economic smallness (even assuming that to be synonymous with independence, which it is usually not), the alternative or supplementary line must be the increasing moralization of bigness. In that direction, whether we like it or not, most indications point. There is, for example, something paradoxical about a state that consistently heads toward bigness in politics, propaganda, finance, debt, armaments, foreign alliances, and commitments, turning round to attack size as such in the economic enterprises within its own borders. It can hardly be argued that bigness on the part of the state has proved safer or more stable in effect than private bigness. It can be argued that bigness in both spheres—or rather, four

9. In this matter of impersonality, the distance between the mechanic on the conveyor belt, the intellectual, the journalist, and the teacher is not so wide. The amount of personal appreciation the columnist or the radio commentator gets for his best work is microscopic compared to the effort he puts in. Have not many of us resolved to send a letter or card of commendation for something that struck us—and failed to do so? Old hands allow for this; but it comes hard on young ones. As an old teacher I was trying recently to estimate the number of students of all ages who must have listened to me, more or less hopefully. It runs well over six thousand. I still hear from a few. What did I mean (if anything) to all the rest? Teachers stay, as it were, on the weir, directing the torrent of young life that comes rushing past them; and what happens to most of it they never know. In that respect their function is not so different from that of the mechanic on the conveyor belt. In both cases, what keeps them going—if they want to be analytic about it—is the inherent worth-whileness of the job, plus perhaps a vague conviction that jobs that get organized on such a scale cannot be lacking in worth-whileness.

spheres if we include organized labor and the co-operatives—has been an ineluctable historical development, constituting the next frontier for civilization. But the civilization must arise mainly from within each group or sector; that is where we differ from the Communists, who would have a superior minority, controlling the state, civilize us all by force.

This maxim, or aspiration, runs counter to the popular view of the state as ringmaster of the economic circus or umpire of the free-for-all—setting the bounds, laying down and enforcing the rules, but otherwise leaving businessmen and lawyers free to fight for their various causes and interests as hard as they can; and let the best man win. The trouble is that, if this is all we have to rely on, it is not necessarily the best man who wins. We are no longer satisfied with this view of the economic process or with its results. On the other hand, we do not wish to see the state running the whole show and telling every participant what to do or not to do; many people hold that we have already gone too far in that direction. The state's proper concern, I have argued, is justice, and that certainly includes the definition and enforcement of rules of procedure. But the coercive power, I have also argued, should be confined to the establishment and maintenance of minimal conditions of both distributive and commutative justice, conditions as to which there exists a very broad basis of moral conviction, because then coercion is hardly felt as coercion. If now large numbers of people wish to advance beyond the social and moral standards thus underwritten, their reliance must be upon voluntary action within and between the functional groups—with outside opinion pushing them on. Not only is this the only way out of the dilemma; it is the most permanently effective mode of procedure, and the only one open to a democracy. It is not dramatic (perhaps we have had enough drama, or melodrama, in recent years), but as applied to present tendencies it raises some interesting questions. shall suggest two of these, closely related.

It is probable that an increasing section of the moder economy is passing from a consumer-controlled to a producer controlled system. Perhaps a hint of this was intended b Professor Slichter's phrase "a laboristic system" as it certainl was by Professor Burnham's book *The Managerial Revolution* This does not mean that the consumer will finally cease to b "king"—short of compulsory rationing, all producers are i competition for the consumer's dollar, and there are elastici ties of demand that cannot be ignored—but the consumer ma have to rule through a constitutional monarchy, including House of Lords. In basic, heavily capitalized, highly organize industry the tendency is plain and would be still plainer bu for the struggles between the upper and lower houses. As w shall see, there are inherent influences making for the sprea of "administered" prices; and among them we must recko the influence of the United States government, which in it many price-pegging and market-control schemes puts the con sumer last, not first. Even in a large part of retail trade, th public is now accustomed to paying prices that are fixed an enforced (without public scrutiny) by private manufacturers this procedure being sanctioned by both state and federal la and Supreme Court decision.

As an "experiment"—to use President Roosevelt's term— in giving associated producers their heads, the NRA has lef no blessed memory. It was an adventure far too reckless rushed into, involving, on the one hand, an ill-advised exemp tion from control and, on the other, an even more ill-advise use of legal coercion. As I have elsewhere pointed out, th functional basis of nearly all the industrial codes was too na row, and the provision for public (presumably consumer) rep resentation was a dead letter. But we must be on our guar against exaggerating the extent to which wishes and theories or even laws and penalties, can determine the development of our social and economic future. If it should appear that producer control over our material destinies is permanently on the increase, then the defects of the NRA, and the claims of alternative schemes, call for careful re-examination. We must in that case seek to discover how, or whether, a satisfactory functional community can be preserved without a limitless increase in either private or public coercion. That is a tougher challenge than any the simple Communist formulas are designed to meet. Indeed, they gain many adherents from people who say it is impossible.

This brings us round to the second, closely related, question. Is it possible that we, or some of our officials, have been making a fetish of competition? The idea that a competitive price is *ipso facto* a just price is a very recent one, and we are still setting limits to its application—limiting, as Sidney Webb used to say, "the plane of competition." But in most other societies we find a certain skepticism, in theory and practice, as to whether competition itself is an adequate vehicle or principle of social justice.

Now that depends in the first instance on what we mean by competition—a matter on which recent court decisions have shed amazingly little light. Much of what goes by the name of competition is essentially a trial-and-error process, an exploratory adventure to ascertain the field for new services, products, or processes; its motive is not strictly or primarily competitive. A good deal more consists in the effort to reduce costs and improve efficiency; and, though we often speak of cost competition, most of this would continue under any system that does not confiscate profits. What the general public understands by competition is aggressive price-cutting. That is a type of economic struggle as to which there is a good deal to be said on both sides; while some laws and many court orders seek to enforce it, other laws (the so-called "fair trade" laws) and court orders seek to restrain it, as do many private business agreements. As a norm of economic conduct, aggressive price-cutting reflects an earlier and more atomistic state of society; today it cannot be assumed that restraint of competition in this sense is *ipso facto* equivalent to restraint of trade. Nor can it be generally assumed, in the sphere of large-scale enterprise, that competition would in any case give a *determinate* answer to the problem of prices.

Modern economic developments, while extremely favorable to the advancement of technique, have not been favorable to the extension of competition. The intricacy of technique itself, resting for the most part on the peculiar nature of American patent law, is a case in point. The enormous increase in capital employed per worker, so strikingly reflected in productivity, tends to shift the emphasis from competition to stabilization. So does the increase in overhead costs of all kinds, especially taxation. So does the workers' demand for pensions and social security. After all, we cannot expect to have it both ways; that is, we cannot at the same time insist on the maintenance of active price competition and pursue policies that increase not only the rigidity of operating costs but the absolute proportion of fixed costs.

It is therefore not surprising, or particularly sinful, that in modern highly capitalized industry, producers tend increasingly to make collective decisions, both national and international; and, the more rigid their costs become, and the more unpredictable their circumstances, the more they will tend to do so. Their quest for security is probably no more dangerous to society than that of the nation-states and a good deal less expensive. When all is said and done, they and their agreements cannot and do not survive except by making and offering goods that an expanding market can afford to buy; and they know by bitter experience that, of all buyers, nation-states are about the worst of risks. Commercial buyers have to earn the means of payment by making, or doing, something useful.

Private business agreements, despite the publicity given them by the Department of Justice, are by no means the dominant feature of American life; they account for neither its best nor its worst aspects.[10] But they do indicate a growing field to which the dogma of competition, in the old sense, can hardly be made to apply; and current efforts to apply it merely illustrate the difficulty. Professor Hamilton, whose great experience in this field gives weight to his opinion, wants more money and more powers for the Antitrust Division, and favors a special type of industrial court to handle all Sherman Act cases. It is remarkable that his book nowhere mentions the Federal Trade Commission, though he states (p. 94) that "a constant oversight, a continuous check, a firm guidance by an administrative agency is essential to turn judicial command into industrial reality."

Some people, however, reflecting on the experience of the last fifteen years in bituminous coal (to say nothing of agriculture), may feel that "firm guidance by an administrative agency" is something we would prefer to escape if we can. As a rule, of course, such guidance is anything but firm; but, even when it is firm, it can claim no unique inspiration. As Professor Hamilton himself has done so much to show, the problems to be dealt with are not simple matters of right and wrong that can be settled by the application of a few elementary principles but extremely complex questions of economic policy that have to be analyzed and debated in the light of the common interest and the long-run effect. While it is reasonable to attribute to administrative agencies a superior degree of detachment, it cannot be assumed, on the evidence of history,

10. Cf. Walton Hamilton's statement (*The Pattern of Competition* [New York: Columbia University Press, 1940], p. 93): "In the economy, as with organic life and human culture, there is no straight line of evolution; nor is there evident anywhere a general trend toward concentration of control."

that their policies or doctrines have any exclusive infallibility. Here as in other cases the extent to which the making of decisions can be safely delegated to the state is painfully circumscribed.

The same conclusion follows on the work of another very competent analyst, Professor A. R. Burns. Burns, like Hamilton, emphasizes the complexity of the economic problems and states frankly that "attempts to restore competition by law offer no prospect of dealing with the developing element of monopolistic control in industry."[11] Nonetheless, almost as if in desperation, he finally comes out with this:

> Administrative bodies able to devote their full time to the making of policy in the control of industry appear to be the best instrument of social control. Legislatures have too wide a variety of activities . . . the judiciary is inappropriate. . . . Bodies representative of all the interests in conflict offer a less satisfactory organ of administration than those consisting as far as possible of impartial persons required to consider the views of the interested parties. In the last resort the kind of policy pursued will be determined largely by the type of person appointed.[12]

Exactly. And that is just what we want to avoid, for we cannot ignore the question of who does the appointing. Confronted by administrative control of that magnitude, we would "rather bear those ills we have than fly to others that we wot not of." The difficulty of getting state administrators to submit their acts and policies to public or even legislative review is at least as great as that of getting businessmen to do so; and they are just as likely to be wrong. Such administrators must and do develop a policy of their own. It may be a very rational one, considered purely as doctrine backed by coercion; but the processes by which actual economic life develops

11. From *The Decline of Competition* by A. R. Burns. 1936. Courtesy of McGraw-Hill Book Co.

12. *Ibid.*, p. 589.

and adapts itself to changing circumstances are too various and too sensitive to be put in a strait jacket.

It by no means follows, for example, that all industrial agreements limiting competition, either national or international, are to be condemned out of hand, even if their result is to keep prices higher than they would be in the absence of any restraint. Practices that are clearly *contra bonos mores* can and should be dealt with on moral grounds, with the co-operation of the trades or industries affected; in this matter American business and government have made an encouraging record of progress over the last thirty years. But, in regard to economic policies that are debatable from the standpoint of public interest, more is to be gained by broadening the basis of debate than by extending the power of coercion. Debate is hardly likely to be free and objective when it is conducted by lawyers and secret police seeking ground for a criminal indictment.

The spread of centralized coercive systems arising from emergency situations has tempted us all to forget that such systems represent a step backward, not forward, on the path of normal development—a reversion toward the sort of state absolutism that every American schoolbook teaches children to regard as "un-American" and a thing of the past. More difficult it is to see that the *type of rationality* by which such systems are necessarily guided is also a step backward; yet we should be able to see that in the light of recent and very ghastly events. The economic structure designed first for Germany and then for all Europe by the leaders of the Third Reich was admirably—yes, devastatingly—logical. It was the product of some of the best technologists in the world; and it was backed, for many of them, by the despairing conviction that nothing but force could achieve so desirable a unification. In that respect we still cannot say with any certainty whether they were right or wrong. But what we did say, in effect, was that, even if they were right, the method was still unwarranted.

Society has to grow into richer and wider forms of communal life by virtue of the development of the mental and moral powers of its own members. That necessity requires that every person, and every association, do his share, and sometimes much more than his share. And what gives history its meaning is that there is always the risk of failure.

X

WHERE LIES SECURITY?

☼

THE cry for security is an instinctive reaction to the appalling insecurity of the modern world. In one way or another—usually in several ways at once—we are all affected by the cumulative insecurity of social, intellectual, political, and economic life that has marked the twentieth century. The psychological as well as the economic results are apparent on every side. Plans for the future of an individual, a family, a firm, a farm, or a nation are confronted by altogether too many unpredictable and uncontrollable factors. Failing any idea, or hope, of a general solution, each seeks some private haven of protection against the vicissitudes of the outside world, including the consequences of similar action by others. The result is a geometrical increase in total insecurity. The demand for security now governs trade-union action at home and largely dictates the promises and policies of politicians; it is also the leitmotiv of our State Department, and of most other state departments, in action abroad. That demand took the United States into both world wars (how much security actually resulted we shall not discuss) and is currently requiring a colossal rearmament. The budgets and programs of almost all Western "powers" reveal the extent to which the national communities have become armed hordes, as in days of old. Not only the European states, but the United States itself, are now in a situation where fear and apprehension, rather than hope and confidence, control their plans, policies, and current expenditures. The result is a quarrelsome congeries of cramped economies and competitive armaments in an era of potential—indeed, actual—abundance; and there are many who tell us that things have to be that way for the sake of—security.

This situation did not arise in a day; it is the achievement of two misguided and greedy generations that deliberately rejected the clue to a human future. But most thoughtful people are agreed that the situation will have to be resolved, or substantially mitigated, in much less time than that. Consistently with the policies, methods, and ideologies of even our own generation, Western civilization and most of the people composing it have not long to live. In no country is the public as much as half-aware of the lethal possibilities. Under present conditions and assumptions the cry for security is a cry for the moon.

Yet security is a good thing, and there is nothing wrong with the demand for more. Even a sure minimum of physical and economic security might release a cultural advance from which, as it were incidentally, further possibilities of security might arise. If the desire for security means that we are willing to slow down the acceleration of our material demands and expectations for the sake of a little more peace of mind (and body), it is a most commendable desire. It does, in practice, mean that, by any calculation. The chances are that we have no real alternative, but our attitude to necessity makes all the difference. This is a case for what Ibsen called "willing what one must." He by no means intended that we should take a fatalistic attitude. What he meant, after wrestling with the human problem at its deeper level (particularly in *Peer Gynt*, *Brand*, and *Emperor and Galilean*), was that our sole salvation lies in finding and accepting the truth about human nature which knows no distinction between the individual and the social at this level—knowing and working with that, not against it; even though we are actually and morally free to work against it, and even though our defiance, in the last accounting, may be put to our credit.[1]

It follows that a large part of our present problem is due to our psychological inability, or reluctance, to face the facts, even though the facts, honestly faced, offer us a better hope of getting out of what we know to be a dead-end street. We are trapped in the psychotic anxiety that afflicts people who are moved by incompatible desires and unable to recognize and cope with the underlying conflict. That conflict may be broadly described as security versus adventure; for one can hardly have both. They connote not only different modes of action but different types of volition.

The systems that have so far defined the outlines of the modern world, internationally or domestically, were on the whole inspired by the psychology of adventure, which accepted a lot of uncertainty and risk-taking along with the chance of big gains and big losses. That psychology still inspires a good deal of American enterprise; but organized labor tends to reject it;[2] and in Europe the tide is distinctly on the ebb. Nowadays, in every sphere, the emphasis is on stability, security, the elimination of risk and uncertainty, the flattening-out of the profit-and-loss extremes, though people still want the results of

1. That was what made Ibsen a great dramatist in the Greek tradition, for the Greeks based their tragedy on that same situation, and of course he knew it. Americans are frightfully apt to assume that politics and culture—this kind of culture—have no integral relation. That is one of the reasons why Europeans, without exception, are afraid of their power. It is worth noting that since Waterloo, with only three exceptions, British premiers have been Oxford or Cambridge men, mostly classicists. It would be naïve to suppose that this is wholly due to class prejudice.

2. An instructive example is currently forthcoming from Mr. Walter Reuther, president of the United Automobile Workers. In May, 1948, the union accepted an agreement which related wage changes to the official cost-of-living index. Under that agreement the union obtained an increase of pay. On July 9, 1949 (*New York Times* special of ensuing date), when the index was showing a downward trend, Mr. Reuther stated that the agreement would be dropped on expiry, because "the union no longer would be willing to accept pay cuts at any time because of decreases in cost of living."

adventure, which in America are usually identified with "progress."

This change of temper is mainly due to the fact that the era of reckless and unco-ordinated expansion—geographical, imperialistic, economic—is now over. At least for the West it is over; and we may well doubt whether the much larger part of the world that is now adopting Western technology will desire to act in as reckless and unco-ordinated a fashion as did the Western states in their expansionist phase. That phase resulted from the hangover of Renaissance statism into the era of modern scientism. We must remember that less than fifty years ago international war was generally accepted, even by liberals, as a normal hazard of the expansionist process; and not only official war, but such all-out struggles as those of the rival munitions and oil interests, with their normal background of politics, bribery and corruption, all the way from the Balkans to Manchuria. We cannot yet say that that sort of thing is definitely over; but we may say that the larger economic and technological interests, driving toward functional organization on an ever widening scale, are increasingly anxious to get rid of it, and eager, when necessary, to surmount the tribal and political fences that get in the way.

But here we encounter an obsession that affects political and professional as well as popular thought. One is tempted to call it a form of the birth trauma that Otto Rank and his followers made so much of. It is the fear of emerging from the small, closed, secure system into the unknown hazards of a larger open system. In comparison with possible future developments in planetary organization, even America is small; she will not be able to have things all her own way. But the necessity of growing up and out from smaller systems into larger systems is the root of social development and intellectual challenge.[3] We may either accept it or be eliminated by it; there is no third way. The transition is always difficult and hazardous, and there have been more failures than successes, tragic failures like that of the Greek city-states and the European nation-states. As crisis approaches, communities are always tempted to raise their fences against the rest of the world, as the Americans did in 1922 and 1930, setting a fatal example to scores of others. We have had time enough to learn that there is no security that way.[4] The younger generation comes knocking at the door, and, if it goes unheeded, it starts knocking with a sledge hammer. The critical distinction lies between policies that welcome the inevitable expansion of the communal area and enlist intelligence, courage, and good will to guide the process, and policies that seek to resist it and stand pat on systems and achievements that seem, but really are not, secure.

One of the facts most frequently forgotten is that by far the greater part of our modern insecurity, economic as well as political, is man-made; it is not in the nature of things. Crop variations and cyclical factors alone would never have piled up to anything like the current degree of instability. Especially after 1919, when a naïve American idealism sanctioned an insane European parochialism, the human factor was in charge and proving unequal to the situation it had itself created. The destruction of the international monetary system, to which Mr. F. D. Roosevelt gave the *coup de grâce*, marked the end of an era; and while many private, and some public, organizations still strove to rebuild a basis of stability, the foundations had been undermined not by natural forces but by human passion, fear, and stupidity.

3. The recent interest in ecumenical organization among the hundreds of national and sectarian religious cults is a significant and encouraging symptom.

4. It is distressing to hear Senator Taft, at this time of day (*New York Times*, September 10, 1949), proclaiming that the restoration of the Reciprocal Trade Agreements Act would give the President "the power to destroy any American industry." Is American industry still a hothouse plant?

The focus and effective vehicle of these vices was beyond question the state itself, and the "successful" conclusion of another war has confirmed rather than weakened the evidence. At the root of our modern insecurity, internal as well as external, is not the division of the world between good states and bad ones but the growing obsolescence of the nation-state itself as an agent of expanding human community. That is one of the reasons—there are many others—why we should hesitate to increase the degree of state control, or state dependence, in any modern community. This does not mean the "withering-away" of the state; even in Marxist theory that idea applies strictly to the state as a coercive organization acting in an interim capacity, pending the realization of spontaneous brotherhood the world over. There are many occasions and objectives as to which a given community needs a central agency to act for it, with a reserve power of coercion, not merely in matters of law enforcement and public order, but in the active promotion of humane and cultural ends. But these are matters in which the aims of a particular community do not conflict but positively harmonize with the similar aims of other communities.[5] Far different is the case—unfortunately, the usual case—where the dominant aims of the state do conflict with the corresponding aims of other states, and this is particularly likely in the materialistic or economic sphere. Indeed, it is the natural characteristic of that sphere.

There are signs in our times, just as there were in the seventeenth century, that thoughtful people engaged professionally in carrying on and extending the economic intercourse of separated communities are aware of the dilemma. It would take

5. The current exchange of schoolteachers between America and Britain is an excellent example. The writer has long wished that an exchange of ballet and choral groups between Russia and America could be arranged, but both governments are too frightened. He likes also to recall the success, and the sheer happiness, of the Anglo-Japanese exhibition at the White City in 1911. Possibly there are some Japanese still living who remember that.

too long to cite them, or even half of them. One has to generalize, and the generalization is properly open to challenge; but here is a sample. There has been much talk, especially in recent Anglo-American conversations, of the expansion of American foreign investment, and there is certainly no innate reluctance on the American end. Two generations ago it was almost a commonplace that the flag followed the Bible and the banker followed the flag. I am not criticizing that procedure; I am merely pointing out that today American foreign investors are not so sure of it. Voluntary foreign investment demands something more than state indorsement (which it has to have) and guaranties, even if they are implicitly backed up by the power of coercion. It has to figure out its own risks and hazards and its own ways of dealing with them; it has to find its own partners (in iniquity, if you choose to put it that way) because state intervention or control in this field no longer counts for much in the way of security—rather the reverse in fact.

In the good old days of British imperialism, investors in the Near East, for example, could take comfort and courage from the safe assumption that Barings' Bank, Lord Cromer, and the British navy and Foreign Office all understood one another and were working as a team for worthy ends. Today it is extremely doubtful whether the advances of the American State Department, backed up by the corresponding advances of such "public" organizations as the Export-Import Bank, the RFC, even the United States Treasury, to Marshal Tito, Marshal Chiang, or who knows whom, either could or should inspire much confidence on the part of the private investor. Times have changed along with money rates, and investment bankers are not so sure of what they will gain by taking the state into partnership. States are not such good risks as they used to be. Indeed, no European "power" (let alone any other) is by itself a good risk. It would be a reasonable and equitable policy, if the American Congress ever recaptured control of American state finances, to require that further openings of the American commercial or financial market be directly related to the degree of tangible progress in the establishment of viable areas or systems. An economically United States of Europe including the Danube Valley would, for example, be a better risk than any comparable area in the Western world and attract American funds on a scale like that of the 1920's—on condition, first, that it were voluntary and therefore reasonably stable and, second, that investors and their agents were free to make their own terms and bargains without having to play favorites in the game of power politics. In the writer's opinion, such a prospect is not so far beyond the bounds of possibility as it seems at present.

It will quite properly be objected that the former experience turned out disastrously. So vivid is the memory that even now it is not easy to market obligations of any foreign state, even the most stable. True, there were not only negligence and carelessness but inexperience and overenthusiasm contributing to the failure of America's first large-scale adventure in private foreign investment. But it must be admitted that public foreign investment during the past decade shows an even worse record—even on the limited amount of evidence that is available. In the former case American foreign investment, broadly speaking (there were some notable exceptions), lacked both an adequate analysis of the economic factors and an over-all policy corresponding to that of Britain in the great days of imperialism—days when one could not tell a banker from a statesman even by his hat. Today American economic foreign policy resembles Eddington's description of the theory of light: Mondays, Wednesdays, and Fridays it is devoted to peace and reconstruction; Tuesdays, Thursdays, and Saturdays it is getting ready for the next world war. That involves a perennial balance or, rather, imbalance of risks, a perpetual insecurity, by which everyone feels thwarted.

Is there any way out of this impasse? There is, I think, one principle that provides a clue. My first senior in the teaching of economics was Alfred Milnes of London. He was an intellectual disciple of J. S. Mill and very much in earnest. He wrote little because he gave all his time and thought to the technique of teaching; so he is not much remembered. In that vocation I received from him an excellent apprenticeship. He had, among other devices, a favorite analogy: when the clay pot of politics and the brass pot of economics go bumping down the river of time, and eventually collide, it is the clay pot that cracks. It needs no argument to show that the logic of economic necessity cannot indefinitely be defied and that, when it is too long ignored, not only economic but political chaos is the consequence.

Speaking from a long-run standpoint, our immediate difficulty is that we cannot see the forest for the trees. The foreground is so cluttered up with short-term arrangements and expedients seeking to rescue a little security, here and there, public or private, from the encroaching world chaos, that we can discern no farther trails. There is, however, at least one—the persistent effort to restore open and untrammeled international markets. Without that effort we have no way of finding out what the underlying economic necessities—and possibilities—are or what kind of relative stability they will dictate. What is economically sensible and feasible has a way of imposing its requirements upon our acts and consciences, but how can we know what it is without a much larger measure of economic freedom than we are allowed at present?

Accordingly, all partial plans for security relating to particular areas, situations, or commodities should be regarded as secondary in principle to the restoration of the open world market. That is the fundamental and primary obligation. Many people, including economists and politicians, have presumed to dismiss the ideal of free trade as romantic or imperialistic humbug. The record of unfree trade is beneath comparison, and the proofs lie on our doorstep. True, the record of free trade was not impeccable, and it entailed big risks on private adventurers; but the record of unfree trade entailed far bigger risks on the political units that took over, far bigger mistakes and losses which they now labor in vain to conceal. Freedom—even, or especially, in economic affairs—is a community-builder, and it has no rival. It is simply meaningless to extol political freedom and disparage economic freedom.

Many of the security plans inaugurated, or revived, since 1924 looked toward economic rationalization, particularly the steel plan of 1926 and certain of the international commodity agreements. Some of them sought to guarantee for years ahead the movement of fixed quantities of goods at fixed prices, or a fixed range of prices, without any assurance of a stable medium of international exchange. Most of them sought in one way or another to overcome the limitations imposed on trade or organization by the various political systems. For many of these agreements there was, and is, a strong case. But, as they sprang from restriction, so they tend to perpetuate restriction. If we could count on a general and steadfast effort to eliminate arbitrary local impediments to trade—including not only excessive tariffs but the innumerable administrative obstacles—and a parallel effort to restore a stable world currency, the conditions of a more normal equilibrium would gradually emerge, and we could go about our planetary mixed farming in the light of a less distorted perspective. No amount of state or interstate planning can contribute as much to stability as this sort of effort, in which every step forward makes the next step easier.

There follows a conclusion of some urgency. Domestic plans and policies, whether public or private, looking toward the regulation of economic life, should be so designed and administered as to avoid arbitrary disruption or interference in the international market. This refers particularly to domestic price-pegging, of which the consequences have been extremely unfortunate. If a state wishes to maintain some group of functionaries at a predetermined level of income or gross revenue, it had far better do so by direct cash subsidy (as in the Brannan plan for American agriculture) than by establishing and supporting price levels that bear no relation to actual supply and demand. The latter policy leads farther and farther away from reality. It drives buyers to other markets, which are usually eager to respond. By curtailing exports, it acts as an additional tariff on all imports and retards the development of foreign trade; it extends the area of internal state dependence, inasmuch as those who rely on the custom of the favored groups are forced (not always unwillingly) to argue for the continuance of the subsidies or protective devices, which in turn leads to some unedifying political manifestations.

This argument for the restoration of open markets is not to be understood without qualification as a plea for the restoration of what statists call the Manchester philosophy, or laissez faire, meaning thereby a combination of planlessness and callousness that rarely existed outside America. The essence of it is that, unless and until the arbitrary obstacles to economic co-operation are removed, we cannot tell where we stand in the nascent wider community, or what natural adjustments and contributions it may require of us all. In matters of major economic import, localism, tribalism, parochialism, feudalism, nationalism, statism, or whatever one chooses to call the backward-looking, backward-longing yearnings for a closed system of security, are relegated to the past—either by way of enlightenment or by way of collapse, war, revolution, and universal privation. The entire world, with no community anywhere excepted (not even Tibet), has been moved too far in the other direction by its scientists, economists, technologists, financiers—and, I think we might add, its philosophers

—in matters, I repeat, of *major* economic import. These matters include the supply and distribution of basic foodstuffs, as to which agronomists now habitually think in world terms; the development of natural power resources, in which political frontiers now rank as a minor nuisance, to be surmounted by any means available; and the exploitation of the planet's limited supply of minerals. The fundamental drive of human intellect, from its peak in mathematical physics to its limitless practical applications, is toward conscious planetary community; and, so long as man is man, it cannot and will not suffer itself to be thwarted. This is our fate, our mortal meaning. It is foolish to ask why. Perhaps there is no "why" in our terms but only a "must." Or perhaps we have to get this job done in order that other possibilities may begin to shine through. What we may be sure of is that we have to achieve as successful a degree of community by voluntary intelligence as other creatures have done by involuntary instinct.

This is no new phase in human affairs; there are plenty of earlier examples of this kind of crisis, most of them pretty discouraging. It seems indeed as if every now and then the dynamic impulse, or destiny, finds itself up against an accumulated crust of confinement, in which historical associations and achievements, accepted customs and small comforts, interests rooted in the "established order," emotional values and intellectual attitudes, are all congealed and embodied. This is the sort of situation that invites ideological (and actual) dynamite.

There are two ways of coping with it—or three, if we include the most general, which is the way of evasion. The way of evasion consists in distinguishing two levels of thought: one to be called abstract or idealistic, respectable but not urgent, entitled to polite approbation on our intellectual Sundays; the other to be called practical, realistic, and accepted as an adequate guide to policy on all other days of the week. It is a significant fact that this method has never amounted to much historically, and it has been consistently disparaged by the great prophets, including Jesus the Christ. We shall therefore waste no more time on it.

Of the two remaining ways of tackling the challenge to wider community, we in America have placed our bet on peaceful and evolutionary processes. We have certainly been influenced by the illusion that we have a monopoly of atomic power; time will dispose of that.[6] But, on the whole, we still incline to believe that the expansion of functional community can be accomplished by peaceful means, and we certainly desire that. We have taken an active part in, and largely financed, the establishment of a whole set of interlinked agencies whose specific charge is the development of economic world community. To a remarkable degree, the world's scientists are in accord as to what should be, and could be, done. There is no lack of resources, provided they are pooled. But there are specific points and areas in which we are required, by our own reasoning, to back our own bet. One, of course, is that of restrictions on trade. Another goes deeper; it challenges our willingness to take a chance on a certain redistribution of the world's resources, in the interests of world community, without waiting for some other party to act first—possibly on less disinterested motives. To be specific, any committee of competent technologists could devise a fairer setup of mineral and transportation facilities, from Kars and Batum to Baluchistan, than what obtains now, provided they were entirely free from internal or external pressures and prejudices and thinking dispassionately in world terms. There are such people; we and other states have gone to a lot of trouble and expense to get them together; and we have not yet been able to get all of them together. But our official credo presupposes that we are willing to follow their advice on the road to world

6. Time did dispose of it on September 23, 1949.

community or at least to accord it considerable weight in our counsels. Summing up at this point, the case is that, if and as we eliminate irrational obstacles to trade and organization, we shall be better able to discern and gradually bring into operation a more natural and rational system from which the element of coercion will tend to disappear; but it is no use talking about the elimination of force if the various societies insist on retaining an economic system so artificial and out of date that only force can keep it going.

We shall not, of course, emerge into the wider field all at once. Progress will be in some matters mainly regional, in others functional; and there may be some social enclaves that must be simply left behind or surrounded. Nor can we decide a priori how much deliberate organization on the bigger scale may be needed. The rule of the open market offers by far the best assurance of flexibility and adaptability; but for capital developments on the modern scale in heavy industry, power, transport, and communications it is logical and necessary that there should be considerable co-ordination of programs and prospects. That co-ordination is the proper function of *capitalists*, not governments or states. Unfortunately, some of the biggest capitalists today are also states, like socialist Britain and nationalist Russia (most of the talk about national or international socialism boiled down in practice to national capitalism), and that fact introduces political and even racial complications into what ought to be a purely functional enterprise. But even in such cases we are not warranted in assuming that the national organization of power will be invoked to block the functional organization of welfare. There is some evidence to the contrary. The crucial issue that all the rest are watching is how we ourselves are going to respond to that temptation. If we reject it, others will take courage; if we succumb to it, the whip of war will once again be laid across our shoulders.

Here, at the end of our colloquy, we encounter the fatal paradox. If we could treat of the state simply as the agent of our spontaneous moral solidarity, we could debate both means and ends within the limits of a common ethos, and use it much or little without deep division. If the agent of our external aims were some other organization, independently devising its policies and techniques for a world where only lethal force avails, we could ignore that for domestic purposes and proceed to construct our private commonweal. Alas, there is and can be no such separation. The agency that acts in the one sphere is the same that dominates the other.

Ten years before the second World War, an English economist of much experience was giving a course of lectures in Boston very similar in theme to these. Having discussed, as I have tried to do, the issues of the day, he ended in precisely the same dilemma.

> All national rights are subordinate to force. . . . The principal cause of war is war itself. War is an industry, and like all other industries involving the use of plant and capital equipment, it requires an interval of time between the beginning of the productive process and its culmination in the delivery of the completed product. The completed product is organized force. . . . Even if war were a visitation comparable to the outbreak of fire, and disconnected with the events preceding it, this question of preparation could not be neglected. The cost of armaments in peace time is often compared to a premium of insurance against fire. The comparison would be more convincing if it did not imply that the fire insurance companies are the principal incendiaries.[7]

That, I repeat, was ten years before the second holocaust. Today I can do no more than echo—a little wearily, perhaps—the warning, for indeed it is possible that mutual destruction is the end and culmination of the human experiment. Perhaps

7. R. G. Hawtrey, *Economic Aspects of Sovereignty* (New York: Longmans, Green & Co., 1930), pp. 81, 97–98.

that is as far as we can go. At least we owe it to ourselves to recognize the possibility.

So long as the practice of organized international war is sanctioned or tolerated, on any ground whatever, it must, it does, and it will dominate every aspect of the economic role of the state; and its domination will increase. What the modern community, with its technical and cultural equipment, might accomplish for itself and for humanity at large surpasses the imagination; for even imagination is circumscribed by the dominant assumption. Thus arises the universal sense of frustration and inhibition, source of so many pathological phenomena; yes, and the sense of guilt, which none who is wholly honest with himself can explain away.

That sense is indeed the ground of our only hope—the only assurance that we should, and can, do better. Our very skills reproach us, for it is not as if we had only lethal skills. The scientists reproach us. The dancers, the poets, the artists, the musicians—all reproach us. Can we be only "free among the dead, like the slain that lie in the grave? . . . A brutish man knoweth not, neither doth a fool understand this."

If we will not, or dare not, renounce the methods of the brute—make the leap into the future which that demands—then nothing that we can say or do or plan will make much difference to our collective destiny. This is no new gospel. But a gospel spurned becomes a doom.

ACKNOWLEDGMENTS

☼

In addition to obligations already noted in the text, I am indebted to the following publishers and/or authors for permission to quote from copyright works: Messrs. Allen and Unwin, London, publishers of *The State and Revolution* by V. I. Lenin; Appleton-Century-Crofts Company, publishers of *Economic Problems of the New Deal* by Atkins, Friedrich, and Wyckoff and of *The Modern Idea of the State* by Hugo Krabbe; the Bruce Publishing Company, publishers of *Weapons for Peace* by T. P. Neill; the Devin-Adair Company, publishers of *The Pope's Plan for Social Reconstruction* by C. P. Bruehl; the B. Herder Company, publishers of *The State in Catholic Thought* by H. A. Rommen; William Hodge and Company, London, publishers of the English translation of *Civitas humana* by Wilhelm Röpke; International Publishers, publishers of *What Is To Be Done?* by V. I. Lenin; Longmans, Green and Company, publishers of *Economic Aspects of Sovereignty* by R. T. Hawtrey and of *The History of Trade Unionism* by Sidney and Beatrice Webb; William Morrow and Company, publishers of *The Treason of the Intellectuals* by Julien Benda (copyright 1928); W. W. Norton and Company, publishers of *Mysticism and Logic* by Bertrand Russell and of *The Modern Theme* by Ortega y Gasset; the Oxford University Press, publishers of *The Modern Democratic State* by A. D. Lindsay. I am also indebted to the editors and proprietors of *Fortune* magazine for permission to reproduce in chapter viii a paragraph from my article, "Business and Ethics," published in their issue of October, 1948.

W. A. O.

SMITH COLLEGE
November 1949

[PRINTED IN U·S·A·]